D-Day,
Arnhem and
the Rhine

D-Day,
Arnhem and
the Rhine

A Glider Pilot's Memoir

Robert F. Ashby

Edited by Jonathan Walker

Pen & Sword
MILITARY

AN IMPRINT OF PEN & SWORD BOOKS LTD
YORKSHIRE – PHILADELPHIA

First published in Great Britain in 2022 by
PEN & SWORD MILITARY
an imprint of Pen & Sword Books Ltd
Yorkshire – Philadelphia

ISBN 978-1-39908-818-3

Typeset by Concept, Huddersfield, West Yorkshire, HD4 5JL.
Printed and bound in England by CPI Group (UK) Ltd, Croydon CR0 4YY.

MIX
Paper from
responsible sources
FSC
www.fsc.org   FSC® C013604

Pen & Sword Books Ltd incorporates the imprints of Aviation, Atlas, Family
History, Fiction, Maritime, Military, Discovery, Politics, History, Archaeology,
Select, Wharncliffe Local History, Wharncliffe True Crime, Military Classics,
Wharncliffe Transport, Leo Cooper, The Praetorian Press, Remember When,
White Owl, Seaforth Publishing and Frontline Books.

For a complete list of Pen & Sword titles please contact
PEN & SWORD BOOKS LTD
47 Church Street, Barnsley, South Yorkshire, S70 2AS, England
E-mail: enquiries@pen-and-sword.co.uk
Website: www.pen-and-sword.co.uk
or
PEN & SWORD BOOKS
1950 Lawrence Rd, Havertown, PA 19083, USA
E-mail: uspen-and-sword@casematepublishers.com
Website: www.penandswordbooks.com

Contents

List of Illustrations

Maps

Plates

Robert Ashby on a motor mechanics course, Norwich, 1940.

Elementary Flying Training School, 1942.

Staff Sergeant Robert Ashby, Glider Pilot Regiment.

A Horsa glider in training.

A Horsa AS.51 being towed into position for take-off.

A General Aircraft Hotspur glider.

Glider pilots in smocks and battledress.

Tugs and gliders take off from RAF Tarrant Rushton.

Sergeant Jim Donaldson.

Anti-glider poles, known as 'Rommel's Asparagus'.

A restored 3-ton Clarkair bulldozer.

Three gliders, containing men of the 6th Airlanding Brigade, land south of the cantilever bridge.

On their wedding day in 1944: Robert Ashby and his bride Jeane.

A Tug towing a Horsa glider.

Arnhem, September 1944.

Airborne troops dig in near the Oosterbeek perimeter.

An anti-tank unit from the 1st Border Regiment firing a 6-pdr gun, recently delivered by a Horsa glider.

A PIAT anti-tank weapon in action with its two-man team.

Generalmajor Friedrich Kussin, commander of German forces in Arnhem, lies dead in his car after being ambushed by 3 PARA, 17 September 1944.

Two sergeants from the Glider Pilot Regiment search ruins in Oosterbeek.

DUKW amphibious vehicles being unloaded.

An M22 Locust light tank disembarking from a Hamilcar glider.

Hamilcar and Horsa gliders and their Halifax tugs prepare for take-off from RAF Woodbridge, March 1945.

Loading a jeep into a Horsa.

US troops crossing the Rhine under fire.

Surrey County Librarian.

Robert Ashby celebrates his 100th birthday with four generations of his family.

Editor's Note and Acknowledgements

The role of personal testimony in military history is valuable. A memoir can provide an antidote to both official histories and lower-level sources, such as battalion or brigade war diaries, though as Robert Ashby readily concedes, his account is a personal experience of action and therefore limited by his immediate surroundings. Nonetheless, his is a very powerful account of three major military operations during the Second World War and his observations and conclusions make compelling reading.

Robert compiled his wartime memoir in the early 1990s, from personal notes and recollections. This was then painstakingly converted into digital format by his son-in-law, Mick Steel. After Robert's death in 2019 his younger son Michael approached me to see whether the memoir might find a wider audience and I was fortunate, through Jamie Wilson and Rupert Harding, to secure Pen & Sword to publish the volume. I have written an introduction, chapter headings and notes to provide both context and additional information, and my text is shown in italics to separate it from the memoir text. I have also drawn maps to illustrate the three major operations in which Robert took part. For the purpose of brevity, the early part of the original memoir, concerning his initial Army training, has been reduced in length.

My sincere thanks to family members Richard and Michael Ashby, Carolyn Steel and Rosalind Thayer for permission to reproduce the work, and for providing background details about their father's life. I am also grateful for the assistance of Simon Tidswell for airborne sources, as well as the Army Flying Museum in Hampshire, a splendid resource for the history of Army aviation. Lastly, my appreciation for the diligent work by Tara Moran and Sarah Cook of Pen & Sword.

Jonathan Walker
April 2022

Robert Frederic Ashby – A Biographical Note

Robert Frederic Ashby was born in 1916, the third child and second son of financial journalist John Frederic and his wife Jessie Milner, a Yorkshire woman. It must be the Yorkshire connection which resulted in his earliest memory, that of sheltering under a table during a Zeppelin raid on Hartlepool. Early years were spent in Harrow and then Watford, where he attended the Grammar School. Leisure was spent exploring the leafy lanes of what was then rural Middlesex and it was an escapade on a motor-cycle which lost him part of a front tooth. Holidays were spent on the Isle of Wight, for which he always retained a great affection. Family financial problems propelled Robert into work, firstly with the local paper manu-facturer John Dickinson and then to Watford Library, where he gained his professional qualification by part-time study, after which he was appointed Librarian and Curator of Hitchin Library. It was while on a placement with a public library in Leipzig in 1936 that he had the unusual experience of seeing Adolf Hitler close up during a handball game.

On the outbreak of war he continued to work until he was called up and entered the Royal Army Service Corps in 1940. When the opportunity came, and with some persistence, he volunteered to become a glider pilot in the newly formed regiment. He learned to fly and was in the first wave of the invasion of continental Europe in Normandy on D-Day at Pegasus Bridge/Operation Tonga. On his return he married our mother Jeane Sells, whom he had first met when she came to change her library books at Hitchin Library. He was at Arnhem, where he narrowly escaped across the Rhine to safety, and was at the final crossing of the Rhine. He was very reticent about his wartime experiences and it was only in the late 1980s that he began to write this account of his army career. Our parents were at the 50th anniversary celebrations of D-Day at Portsmouth and were interviewed in the media coverage of the day. They contributed some memorabilia to the D-Day Museum at Southsea.

Never one to seek preferment, Robert declined the offer of a commission and in 1945 returned to civilian life with a resumption of the job in Hitchin Library and the beginning of family life with the birth of two sons and then two daughters.

In 1950 Robert Ashby was appointed Librarian and Curator in the Borough of Kettering but in 1953 the family moved to Surrey, where he became deputy County Librarian. Four years later he was appointed County Librarian, a post he held until he retired in 1977. He presided over the transformation of the library service into a thoroughly professionalised and progressive organisation. He sat on national committees, chaired the Society of County Librarians, was on the Library Advisory Council and was sent by the British Council to Italy and Nigeria to advise on library development.

Robert's great passion was for books, and it is a passion he passed on. Earliest family memories are of sitting in an armchair with our father reading to us. No doubt this is also one of the earliest memories of his grandchildren, in whom he took great pleasure and pride. He was a great book collector, couldn't resist a second-hand bookshop, and built up a fine collection of first editions of the obscure Suffolk poet Robert Bloomfield.

He was also a very practical man, making our Christmas presents in the early 1950s. His rather illogical training as a mechanic in the army was finally put to some use and he spent endless hours underneath the succession of old cars – all that could be afforded at the time. He built a canoe and a Mirror dinghy and two of his children developed a lifelong love of sailing and met their partners this way. He taught himself bricklaying and electrical wiring and after retirement he largely taught himself bookbinding. There are books bound by him on the shelves of the Chichester Cathedral Library, where he worked as a volunteer for some years.

In 1980 he and Jeane moved for a final time to West Sussex. He celebrated his 100th birthday in the company of four generations of his family in the residential home to which he had moved after a fall. He died in December 2019 at the age of 103.

Richard Ashby
Michael Ashby
Carolyn Steel
Rosalind Thayer

Introduction

Today, the military glider has vanished from the battlefield, eclipsed by the helicopter and made redundant by the widespread use of radar. But for a few brief years during the Second World War the glider seemed to provide the answer to delivering units of up to twenty-eight specially trained 'airlanding troops', or heavier equipment, to one landing zone, hopefully with the element of surprise. Paratroops were then still an essential part of airborne operations, but navigation errors or wind direction could spread them far and wide beyond the target. It was also difficult to drop their assault equipment by parachute, including light anti-tank guns, Bren-gun carriers and jeeps, and even if it were possible, they too would end up some distance from their gun teams and drivers. The glider, meanwhile, was deemed a cheap and expendable 'packing crate', but their crews were not. Army glider pilots were in fact highly trained fliers and as competent and brave as their Royal Air Force counterparts. In fact, their role extended beyond flying, for after they had negotiated a perilous landing, they were then often required to fight on the ground alongside the units they had delivered.

The men of the Glider Pilot Regiment were therefore both skilled and resourceful, and their occasional memoirs have enriched post-war research. This remarkable new memoir by one of their number, Robert Ashby, not only adds to this archive, but brings a new and fascinating angle to our understanding of airborne operations. By his own admission, he was not imbued with martial spirit and this makes his narrative and observations all the more unique. For he casts a critical eye over some of his fellow soldiers, his superiors, and certainly their conduct during combat – his involvement in three of the largest glider operations in the Second World War allows him to speak with some authority.

Robert Ashby flew a variety of aircraft and gliders in his training and in action but had most experience with the Horsa glider. His learning curve was rapid, as was the development of such gliders, for they had only just appeared in military operations in the early months of the war. On 10 May 1940 the Nazis invaded the Low Countries and launched the first ever glider-borne operation against the formidable Belgian Fort Eben-Emael. The assault was a success, and it alarmed the new Prime Minister Winston Churchill, who put his weight behind the formation of a similar British force of shock-troops. In early 1942 the Parachute Regiment and the Glider Pilot Regiment were formed as part of the Army Air Corps.

The first few British glider operations were not a success. Operation Freshman in November 1942 dispatched two Horsa gliders with sappers (attached to the 1st Airborne Division) to sabotage a heavy water plant in Norway. They crashed due to bad weather and all the men, including the glider pilots, either died in the landings or were later executed under Hitler's notorious commando execution order. Then in July 1943 the much larger Operation Husky saw the Horsa and the more compact Waco glider used in the invasion of Sicily. However, inexperience and poor navigation from the towing aircraft resulted in high numbers of gliders crashing short into the sea or landing wide of their targets. Large casualties meant many questioned the future of the glider.

But Operation Overlord and the D-Day landings finally proved the worth of gliders. In the right circumstances and with the proper training of crews, they could deliver small units of men and allow them to attack specific enemy targets with a coup de main (speed and surprise), as well as putting larger infantry units and their equipment into tight areas. Despite their undoubted successes, this was an exercise that paratroops always struggled to master.

As he readily admits, he was fortunate to miss the first two disastrous glider operations, but it was D-Day that proved to be his baptism of fire. However, some three months after Normandy, he was again in a perilous situation when he took part in the Arnhem operation, popularly now known as 'A Bridge Too Far'. He reminds us that British glider pilots were unique in that once they had landed their glider, they fought as infantry, and at Arnhem that was a tough proposition. In vivid prose, he contradicts the assessments of official reports on the battle and condemns the memoirs of senior commanders that talk of 'organised retreat'. Being in the thick of the fight, he was well qualified to comment.

In March 1945, as the Allies were poised to take the war onto German soil, he was involved in the Crossing of the Rhine, the largest airborne operation ever mounted on a single day in one place. From a modern standpoint, it is easy to assume that by the early months of 1945, the Allies had such a momentum that their victory was assured. Furthermore, it is also taken for granted that their soldiers must have felt that, with the end in sight, their chances of returning home safely were infinitely higher. But the reality, as Robert Ashby reminds us, was different. The shock of the sudden German offensive in the Ardennes in the winter of 1944/45, together with the real-isation that the Germans would now be fighting for their homeland rather than occupied territory, instilled a certain fear within Allied soldiers. Nothing, including a future life, would be taken for granted in the final operations. From Robert's account, we learn that for airborne forces and their pilots, the first hours of Operation Varsity were horrific, and he was indeed fortunate to survive. Overall, the odds for these glider pilots were poor and by the end of the war, 592 young men of the Glider Pilot Regiment had died in the service of their country.

Before becoming a glider pilot, Robert enlisted in the Royal Army Service Corps (RASC). He describes his initial training, giving us a fascinating insight into his fellow ranks as well as the NCOs and officers, and refresh-ingly observes that some of those in command did not always earn respect. Clearly unimpressed with the military machine, he dissects the monotonous aspects of a soldier's routine and questions the purpose of endless travelling between different depots and camps. He provides the reader with many amusing anecdotes – some reinforcing the caricature of the bellowing sergeant major. Consequently, the RASC held little attraction for him and it was no surprise that when the opportunity arose to join a more technical and innovative branch of the Army, he was keen to leave.

He began his Army flying by training on a Tiger Moth, reminding us how flight was a unique experience in the early years of the war, long before package holidays made most people familiar with this form of travel. He leaves us in no doubt that flying these machines was a tricky business, and gliders particularly required great stamina and concentration to control. They also required pilots to have vision acuity, depth perception and balance. Great concentration was required to keep the tow rope tight for if it slackened too much, the rope could twist around a wing and rip it away. The glider had to be kept slightly above or slightly below the towing aircraft (tug). If the glider followed the tug in exactly the same flight path, the glider would hit air turbulence, which could snap the tow rope. Communication between the tow-tug and the glider was via a telephone cable inserted in the tow rope.[1]

Unlike fighter or bomber pilots, glider pilots were not issued with para-chutes. In a throwback to the First World War mindset, it was felt that if they were issued, the pilots might too easily abandon their cargoes. How-ever, none of the twenty-eight 'airlanding' infantrymen they carried was issued with a parachute either – an inflatable vest, should the glider ditch in water, was thought sufficient. Neither did the glider have any defensive weapons, so it was subject to both air and ground fire. There was a further risk and it didn't involve the enemy. If the glider load contained anti-tank guns, jeeps or other equipment, it was vital that these were properly secured before take-off. If they broke loose in flight, as sometimes happened, it was disastrous – sliding backwards they would rip out the rear fuselage, or moving forward they would crash through the pilots' cockpit with inevitable results.

During the flight there was none of the peaceful 'swishing' of a modern civilian glider, and it was so noisy in the fuselage that no one spoke – they just smoked or contemplated the mission. If there was no enemy flak, there was a certain peace when the glider pilot released the tow rope, but the descent was often quick and dramatic. Military gliders fell, rather than floating around and gaining lift from thermals. Coming in to land at approximately 70mph, the flaps enabled the glider to keep a steady speed to avoid stalling, but landing was hugely variable, depending on the weight of the glider's cargo, the condition of the ground and the obstacles it encoun-tered. With the Horsa glider, the landing gear might remain on landing but generally it was ripped off and the skid rail underneath took the impact. The level and firm landing zone the pilots were promised rarely materialised, for there were many hazards such as ditches, hedges and trees to contend with. In addition, man-made obstacles such as fences, telephone and electric wires often crossed the fields. Wandering livestock were unpredictable and pilots also had to contend with other troops and vehicles disembarking or forming up, as well as the wounded lying in the zone. And there was always the possibility that paratroops from an adjacent drop zone would drift and land in amongst the gliders in a landing zone.

After the shock of landing, airlanding troops would rapidly disembark, or, if there were guns or jeeps in the fuselage, the cockpit would be swung open to allow access. Alternatively, the tail section could be unbolted (or if stuck, blown off with a cartridge) and with the aid of runner rails, the equipment was rolled down. All this could take place under fire, so it was vital that if a vehicle was part of the cargo, its engine was already running when the glider hit the ground, to ensure a quick drive away. Once the troops had disembarked, or the vehicles and guns had been removed, the glider pilots were ordered to move forward into the action and fight as infantry until ordered to retire and somehow make their way out of the battlefield.[2]

These drills would be applied to all gliders, but Robert Ashby spent most of his Army career flying the Horsa. This iconic aircraft was originally constructed by the Airspeed factory in Portsmouth, but, as demand grew, furniture manufacturers such as Lebus were drafted in to make the plywood and timber fuselage sections, which were then bolted together, canvassed and finished off by RAF maintenance workshops. The Horsa, together with the other British gliders, the Hotspur, Hamilcar and Hadrian, were all named after military leaders prefixed with the letter 'H'.[3] *The early AS.51 Mark I Horsa had a fixed pilot cockpit and, just behind it on the port side, a wide fold-down door, allowing jeeps and guns to be loaded and unloaded. Troops entered by a sliding door within this contraption. The AS.58 Mark II improved things by letting the whole cockpit swing out, permitting loading and unloading to take place from the larger front section of the fuselage. Access was also available by unbolting the tail section – useful if the front of the glider had smashed on landing.*[4]

As an experienced flier, Robert was always the 1st pilot and therefore responsible for the take-off, flight and landing, while he was assisted by a succession of 2nd pilots who oversaw the loading of vehicles and equipment as well as flight and landing navigation.

He was relieved when the war ended and he could return to his professional career and progress to become County Librarian for Surrey. While he missed the camaraderie of the Army, he was never an enthusiast for military ceremony and felt that his regimental association's post-war reunions were best left to others. As with most regimental associations, the dwindling number of veterans resulted in the closure of the Glider Pilot Regimental Association in 2016, but fortunately the torch of remembrance was lifted by a group of remaining veterans, their families and enthusiasts, who have recently formed a new civilian organisation called the Glider Pilot Regiment Society.[5]

As for the gliders, they faced a limited future. Less than 5 per cent of all gliders used were ever retrieved from landing zones. The glider carcasses on the battlefields were sometimes cut up by local inhabitants and used as *caravans or garden huts, while the large number of unused gliders, particularly in the US, were sold off for as little as $75 each. By the time of the Korean War in 1950, the use of military gliders in combat operations had all but ceased and the last British troop-carrying glider was withdrawn from service in 1957.*

In retirement Robert did visit the scene of his wartime dramas at Arnhem and Normandy and there were occasions when some of his military adventures found their way into newspaper articles.[6] As he confirms in his epilogue, he recognised that the cause was just but he was often disillusioned by the way military operations were executed. Post-war, he was happy to return to his family, resume his career and record the memoirs of a modest but very brave 'citizen soldier'.

Chapter 1

Beginnings – Joining the Royal Army Service Corps

For the purposes of this memoir it is only necessary to say that at the time it begins I was a chartered librarian in the post of librarian and curator at Hitchin in Hertfordshire. My parents lived at Watford where I had been to school and where I started my library career. Apart from the educational background and specialised qualifications required for my job, I had some fluency in German, having visited the country in 1934 and lived and worked in it for two months in 1936.

My military career may be said to have begun when I was summoned to appear for a medical examination and some sort of selection procedure at a public hall in St Albans. Earlier I had registered, as was required, at a Labour Exchange as part of the conscription arrangements.

The 'medical' was superficial: presumably I showed no outward sign of physical disability. In fact I was quite fit. I was then a few months short of my twenty-fourth birthday. The interview was with an officer of about my own age. I had little knowledge of the Army, and it has been some wonder to me since that, considering what a radical, and as it turned out lengthy, alteration it made to the direction of my life, I did not enquire further into possibilities and potentialities. No one, even my father, who had been in the Army in the First World War, gave me any useful advice. The whole idea of going to the wars had, in this spring of 1940, something unreal about it.

There had been some discussions at home about what one should do about being called up. It was vaguely thought that one should, if possible, avoid the infantry – the poor bloody infantry. We had heard, however, that there was a branch of the Army called the Royal Army Service Corps (RASC) which was concerned with transport. I could drive a car and owned a motorcycle, together with knowledge of how they both worked. Driving around sounded better than sitting in a trench or serving a gun.

So I opted for the RASC on my registration form, little thinking that the authorities would take notice of my preference.[1]

I believe my interviewing officer was from the RASC but I was too ignorant to tell from his badges. He was surprised I was not going for a commission, bringing into the argument the Rotary Club Wheel, which I happened to have in my lapel. I needed to say, however, that I had driven a van or lorry of some kind. Being then somewhat of a George Washington turn of mind I could not so declare. In any case, I had thought of the question of a commission but had decided against it. I was not militarily minded (rather the other way in fact) and with my unimpressive height of five foot six inches and a conciliatory manner, I did not think I possessed that elusive attribute, OLQ (officer-like quality), which was supposed to be required. I also felt that before I presumed to direct others in battle I had better find out how I reacted to it myself. I was content to start at the lowest level.

So, on 15 March 1940, I found myself on a train bearing me away from my normal life into a distinctly abnormal one. I had not, and I do not think others had, any idea what a division between an old existence and a new one this railway journey meant.

There had been no particular ceremonial or expression of regret at my departure except from my nearest and dearest who, like me, visualised no long separation. Compared with what one reads of the send-off of troops in previous wars, with flag-waving and brass bands, my departure was definitely low-key. The whole event was little different from going off on a short holiday and I even left personal possessions in the desk drawer in my office, not thinking that from that day of departure I had no further status there, nor would have for another six years.

On my way to the station I called in to say goodbye to my old chairman of committee, Mr William Payne, a Quaker dentist in Hitchin. It was a courtesy call and I perhaps hoped he would give me the sort of blessing, if any, that Quakers usually give. Among other things he said, 'Well, Mr Ashby, is there anything more we need to discuss for the library committee next Friday?' He was dead before I had anything to do with committees again.

The place to which I was bidden to report was Sudbury, Suffolk. At the station were assembled about eight or nine young men, equally awkward and uneasy, the first batch of conscripts to be posted to the unit. An open lorry came into the yard and, with no greeting and very few words, in the impersonal way that was typical of the Army then, it was indicated that we should climb in. We were conveyed to a pokey old shop in a back street in the town. It was here that I first learned a basic fact of Army life: that, unless one is actually in a campaign, time is of no consequence. The Army has an endless amount of it, far too much to be productively employed. Thus both the individual and the organisation have to find shifts to get rid of it, one of which is to spin out all activities to the greatest possible length at the slowest possible pace. My naive mind had imagined that, with the nation embattled and the flower of the nation's youth (including me) called to the colours, there would have been some sense of urgency in preparing for the coming fray. There was absolutely none.

So we were just sat down on backless benches in the dark little shop and for a long time no one said anything to us. Then we were called up to a clerk one by one and, in a bored and off-hand manner, had our particulars duly registered, including religion and next of kin. I cannot remember if we were given food or drink but I suppose we must have been. Eventually, without explanation, we were put into a truck again and driven to Long Melford. Down a narrow yard was what had been a horse-hair cloth factory. This was to be our home for a couple of months or so.

The unit to which I had been called up was the 534 Divisional Ammunition Company, RASC, soon to be renamed the 54th Division Ammunition Company. It was, or had been, a territorial unit based at Luton. Presumably it had been mobilised in September 1939, so that in March 1940 its existence as an operational unit had extended over little more than six months. It was composed, as one would expect, mainly of motor mechanics and van drivers, though, perhaps oddly, I cannot be sure of this. Although there was ample time and opportunity for talk, reference was seldom made to one's civilian background. This seemed to be part of the Army's convention. There was a sprinkling of more educated people in the ranks, especially in the company office to deal with the paperwork. Some of the officers had been car salesmen or something else in the motor trade, and I believe the overall commander of the divisional RASC, which had other companies engaged in transporting petrol and other stores, was the owner of a garage business.

The sleeping accommodation of our billet was a long narrow upper room reached by an iron outside staircase. It had formerly held the looms upon which the horse-hair fabric had been woven. The floor was rough plank, the windows casement-type with small panes, some of them broken, and there was no ceiling. All was old and shabby. There were about twenty wood and canvas beds. I do not recall mattresses, and there were certainly no sheets. The bed clothes consisted solely of rough grey Army blankets. Pyjamas, then and later, were never seen. We slept in our underclothes, and in very cold weather in our shirts too, with our great-coats on top of the blankets.

Whilst on these domestic matters a word on such necessary facilities as the toilet arrangements must not be omitted. Initially to us gently brought-up civilians who had been taught always to lock the door, they administered a shock to the nervous system greater than all else. Behind the mess room and past the Soyer stoves was a row of stalls, constructed of wood, roofed but open at the front and sides. Each contained a wooden lavatory seat with a tall tubular bucket below. Even to one who had attended Boy Scout camps the lack of privacy was alarming. But for the first few occasions only. After this it was quite pleasant to spend ten minutes or so 'on the bog', musing on the stretch of Suffolk countryside (we were on the banks of a small stream which runs parallel to Long Melford's main street) and engaging in light and doubtless Rabelaisian conversation with people in nearby stalls similarly occupied.

Of course the buckets soon got filled up with all-too-visible human ordure. They had to be emptied into a cess-pit by those of us whose turn had come to be 'on fatigue' as 'shit-house wallah'. This like anything else had to be taken as a matter of course – there was no question of demur-ring – and got over as early in the morning as possible before the main body were stirring. The buckets had to be washed out in cold water. If disinfectant was used, I cannot remember it.

The normal day's work started with a parade and inspection which was held in Long Melford High Street in full view of the local citizens. For the first few morning parades we newcomers turned out in our civilian clothes, which must have looked grotesque among our uniformed com-rades. After a day or two and much waiting about outside the quarter-master's stores, we gradually got kitted out with all the Army in its wisdom considered we required. There was mostly two of everything: two sets of khaki serge battledress (a garment consisting of blouse and trousers which overlapped only at the waist, leaving lumbar regions rather cold) and two pairs of heavy black leather boots, together with shorts, socks and under-wear, non-elastic braces, shaving kit in a cloth roll and even a 'housewife' or 'huzziff' containing needle, thread and spare brass buttons. The clothes and especially the khaki serge were very rough and irritating.

Unfortunately, the resources of the 'Q-stores' were limited and no trousers could be found to fit me; they were promised for later. Rather than make myself a scarecrow, I presented myself on the next parade in my usual civilian garb, thereby incurring a rebuke. I recalled, and I think the inspecting officer did too, that one of the forms of protest used by conscientious objectors was refusal to put on uniform. Thus until the trousers came I paraded in full military uniform apart from a pair of grey flannel slacks.

Inspections were a daily occurrence and I never ceased to resent them. The officer would stare into your face at close quarters to examine the quality of one's shave or ascertain if one had shaved at all. I was once told I had used a blunt razor. Hair had to be short, all the little brass accoutrements of our belts and straps bright, the cap badge and the toes of one's boots brilliant. I was allotted, doubtless because the standard straps and belt of webbing equipment were not available at first, two hard leather Bren-gun ammunition pouches (there were no Bren-guns within miles) which hung on one's chest like large rectangular breasts. As they were brand new, it seemed to my simple mind that they required little cleaning: I was reprimanded for not cleaning them.

The kit consisted of a backpack, a haversack dangling on one's right side with a water bottle on the other, all fixed to shoulder straps or the belt by brass buckles. This was 'full marching order'. In 'battle order' the pack was left behind and the haversack carried on one's back, its place on the belt filled by a variety of other gadgets. All these items, together with the gaiters which closed the gap between the boots and trouser-ends, had to be blanco'd green. Blanco was a clay-like substance which was mixed with water and brushed into the stiff webbing fabric, thereafter being left to dry. The long great coat had a large number of brass buttons, to help polish which without soiling the cloth one was issued with a 'button stick', a piece of slotted brass. Attending to the lustre of the buttons, buckles and tabs on the various items of equipment and trying to get a mirror-like finish on the toecaps of the deeply-grained leather boots occupied most of the evenings. Some of the old soldiers did really use 'spit and polish' on their boots.

Training consisted of foot-drill and marching, which followed on from morning parade. Our parade ground was an area of tarmac on the edge of Long Melford's village green. It was conveniently opposite the school, so that the children could be diverted by our blundering efforts to right-turn and left-turn, and, most difficult of all, about-turn. As soon as we could distinguish left from right and all the time remember which was which, we became very proficient. Our marching drew compliments, not to us but to our drill corporal. I remember once, as 'right marker' leading the squad of perhaps thirty men in column of threes gloriously down the middle of the High Street, boots crunching, arms swinging from the shoulder, when my cap – that extraordinarily designed forage cap, then the norm for both Army and RAF – began to slip off. Not to break the rhythm I let it do so and someone at the rear picked it up. This conduct, though correct, was regarded as perhaps overdoing it a little.

Parades were a basic part of life. We paraded for everything – for going bathing (we must have had baths, though I do not remember where), for the issue of kit and equipment, for inoculations and for medical inspection. Of the last, which happened not infrequently, there was an embarrassing one colloquially entitled 'short-arm inspection' where the MO (Medical Officer) looked to see if one had the outward and visible signs of VD. On one of these the doctor commented scathingly on the manner in which circumcision had been performed on me, 'a bad bit of cobbling that!', he remarked. The point had never occurred to me before, and in any case was hardly my fault.

After some weeks had passed, and at a time when I suppose we were considered proficient in foot drill, we were issued with rifles. These were the Short Lee-Enfields which had been standard in the First World War. Stories circulated of sons being given the same rifle, identified by its individual number, as that used by their fathers. Such a coincidence might have occurred but I doubt it. The arrival of the rifles was not an unmixed blessing. Certainly it made us feel that we had got a step further on the road to being proper soldiers, but it was one more piece of equipment to look after, and with its sling, one more piece of webbing to be blanco'd. It also required a drill which was more complicated and arduous than foot drill.

Early, we went through the instruction called 'the naming of the parts'. Bent and sear, upper and lower swivel and of course the bolt, which always had to be 'clean, bright and lightly oiled' were committed to our memory. We had dummy .303 rounds to load and unload: of live ammunition there was none. I can't remember when I first fired a real live shot, but it was probably about a year later, although at some period we had access to a rifle which had been adapted to fire 0.22 cartridges. I always enjoyed rifle firing: I was good at it.

The drill was instilled into us in the exact words of the Army manual: 'Cant the rifle across the body with the right hand and seize it with the left below the upper sling swivel' was (approximately) the first movement to bring one's position from 'order arms' to the 'slope'. The rifle was a heavy object and difficult to keep at the correct angle. Once, later on, when the company sergeant major (CSM) was having one of his weekly parades, and we had been issued with bayonets, the long sword-bayonet type, the drill for which we were also practised in (e.g. 'When I say "fix", ye don't fix. When I say "bayonet", ye whip 'em out and whop 'em on!'), the whole company was standing at the slope when the CSM summoned me out of the ranks. 'What do you think of that man's slope?' he asked, pointing to the victim intended. 'Very bad, sir,' I replied. 'And what about that one?' 'Awful, sir,' I said, entering into the spirit of his little joke. 'Well, you look ten times worse than either of them – return to the ranks!'[2]

Rifle drill, foot drill and marching made up a good deal of our early training and as we became proficient they even became enjoyable. I suppose the experience was not dissimilar to that of members of a choir or orchestra, one's individuality sunk in a common creative act.

Within a fortnight or so of my joining up I was told I was to be a dispatch rider (DR). This arose from the fact, I think, that in the company there was a man I had known at school and seen occasionally in Watford afterwards. He was a full two-stripe corporal and being thus one of lower management had evidently put a good word in for me. The relationship between people in the Army was very subtle. With one's equals one was a fellow-sufferer in the same cause. We would help each other out in small ways and share our dislike of those in authority. With those above, i.e. corporals and sergeants, who were a race apart, and with those in positions of quasi-authority like the clerks in the orderly room or the cooks, if you were 'known' you got a more friendly deal than if you were not. This could materialise in perhaps a better helping of meat, an earlier leave pass or a better-fitting battle dress. This rapport was not to be contrived;

it emerged usually from some casual shared experience, such as a drink or a journey taken together, which established a personal relationship. It was the ranker's equivalent of the 'old boy network'. Of course there were others with whom you developed an antipathy at sight: you kept out of the way of them.

The personalities which had the greatest significance for us were of course the sergeants and the officers, in that order. The sergeants were a very varied lot and, looking back, I can say that whilst most had to be treated with caution, they generally were at least good-humoured. I never met the Hollywood-type 'bucko' or man-hating sergeant who drove people to suicide. Most were distant, firm and somewhat rough, and though their language was often fruity, both on and off parade, it rarely descended to a lower level than the 'you 'orrible little man' type of insult. They were sufficiently human for songs to be made up about them, an attention which they undoubtedly enjoyed. The sergeant majors, of which there were two in our unit, were redoubtable figures with whom one had communication only on certain occasions such as the one I have described.

Below the sergeants there were the lance-corporals and corporals, people on the way up, who, as they lived amongst us, were largely known to ourselves. They were not accustomed to power and were sometimes cautious in using it. They would, for instance, hold back all the passes if an individual among us had not completed some job or other, even if it meant everyone missing an infrequent bus, but their main function was to lead small working parties. People on the company office or stores often had 'protection stripes' to give them authority solely within their own domain.

Of the officers it is difficult for me to write dispassionately. It was often hard to see what special gifts they had which qualified them for their rank. Some of them had occupied very minor roles in 'civvy street' and having for the first time obtained status by bluffing their way into a commission were determined to hold on to it and improve it by whatever means. Their main anxiety, as I saw it, was to keep up their position; and they did this by their different dress and by their arrogant and insolent behaviour to all below them. The main weapon of the ambitious ones was a hectoring insolence. I learnt later that they suffered the same themselves from their own superiors. They were very keen on being saluted – this could be a bit complicated if one was carrying anything or, as an 'other rank', standing to attention when being addressed. To fail to do so was a military crime. One had to salute flags on staff cars too. I heard of one general who had a posse of followers to pick up the negligent or short-sighted. Thus were 'discipline' and 'bearing' maintained.

In spite of the conventional assumption that all officers are gallant, just as all soldiers are bold, all Jack Tars jolly and airmen intrepid, experience showed that some were not. As for leadership quality, whatever that is, I rarely met one who had it. After the war I was present when two of my co-ævals were recalling boastfully, for my benefit, that each had 'been commissioned as an officer in His Majesty's Forces' and had learnt how to handle men (the erotic overtones of the phrase had not struck them). I reflected that it could not have taken exceptional personal qualities to get one's orders obeyed with the weight of the Army Act, and all the power and privilege that went with a commission, behind one. But that is not leadership. As for officers who were 'worshipped by their men', I never met one, nor do I think anyone else did, outside of obituary notices.

Suffolk is a beautiful, gentle county still; in those days it was quite remote, very agricultural and with little traffic. It was spring: sometimes the clear keen air and wide vault of heaven seemed to have a special quality which, if I meet something similar now, I still call 'a Long Melford morning'.

After 2000 hours we could go out into the village but not away from it. There was not in fact anywhere much to go. In these early days communities had not organised themselves to be hospitable to the conscripted guests in their midst; there were no canteens in the village halls or 'quiet rooms' (complete with darts and radio!) in the vicarage. Navy, Army and Air Force Institutes (NAAFI), the Forces' principal resort in off-duty hours, was nowhere near Long Melford.[3] So there was only the pub or remaining in one's bed. Soldiers had not money enough to go to the pub except occasionally and they saved what they had for a good night out at the end of the week.

Any soldier could be stopped by military police, or indeed anyone of superior rank, and asked for his pass. If he had not got one, he was absent without leave (AWOL), liable to arrest and likely to be charged. Being 'charged' was a perpetual hazard. There was a section of the Army Act (Section 64 I think) under which one could be arrested for 'conduct to the prejudice of good order and military discipline'. This covered everything from having a bootlace undone (being 'improperly dressed'), to failure to obey an order. Arrest was usually 'open'; 'close arrest' was for conduct which would be regarded as criminal in 'civvy street'.

Every morning there would be a 'defaulters parade' outside the company office when the accused, with much shouting and stamping of feet, would be marched before the officer commanding. As a sign of disgrace, the defaulter had to have his hat off, sometimes knocked off by the sergeant major. The charge would be read out, explanations asked for, and a guilty verdict invariably given (not to do so would undermine the authority of him who had brought the charge). The penalty was usually in terms of confinement to barracks (CB) for a varying number of days.

I am trying to show what it was like to be in HM Forces at this juncture. To conclude, I will attempt to describe how I felt about it. I still remember my emotions after nearly fifty years. Although I was a conscript, I had no great resentment about being called up. I was single and unattached and, in many ways, looked forward to service life as a new experience, perhaps an adventure, As Dr Johnson said, 'Every man thinks meanly of himself for not having been a soldier.' I regretted the interruption in my career which I had thought was by then well established but had no doubt that the war was no more than a temporary interruption and that I would soon be back. I also assumed that the Army, having called me into its service, would make some effort to develop, or at least employ usefully, such small abilities as I had. That in some ways would constitute their side of the contract.

However, what I had not bargained for was the entire loss of personal liberty and indeed of personal dignity. The Army had you at its own arbitrary disposal and at this time there was an undefined assumption that the private soldier was either feeble-minded or potentially delinquent or both. Consequently, it kept you in a tight grip. It had the power to make you do this or that, however unpleasant or grotesque or illogical, or to go here or there, without explanation or any apparent reason. Once in, there was no getting away from it, either by day or by night. To be off-duty was to be not free but on a leash, restricted to time and place. Even when at home on leave (to which one had, I believe, no entitlement, its correct term being 'privilege leave'), the Army could recall you at a moment's notice – this happened to me twice.

There was nothing to be proud about in being in the ranks of the British Army. How different in Germany, where a man thought less of himself, and was thought less of by others, if he had never been a soldier. One soon found that on joining the ranks, one became de-classed. Relegated to the lowest level of the social pyramid, one was no longer a person but a soldier, and everyone knew what soldiers were like. This was conveyed in subtle ways. The accustomed courtesies, the normal attention from waiters, shop people, bus conductors and the like, which were much more in evidence at that period than today, was of lowest quality, sometimes verging on the contemptuous. The better establishments were 'out of bounds to other ranks' or for 'officers only'. One gravitated insensibly towards the down-town pub, the workman's cafe, the Salvation Army Canteen. One found people there who did not resent one's presence.

To this process the ill-fitting 'battle dress' with its tie-less collar, the heavy boots and the ridiculous cap contributed. When the Americans arrived, the fact that the lowliest GI (General Infantryman) had a better uniform than ours was an important factor in giving him a status which was higher than that of any one of us below commissioned rank. It created great resentment.

It was true, however, that the common soldier all too often tended to merit the inferior position allotted to him. Some were in fact very common indeed. I well remember my first night in the horse-hair factory. It was a Friday and the men had been allowed out late. We newcomers had gone to bed about 2200 hours and an hour later the rest of the billet came in. They were not drunk but, as they say, had drink taken. Their exuberant high spirits burst out into the most lurid backchat I had ever heard, the subject being whether and how far and in what way some of their number had got on with their female companions. I and my compeers were not ignorant of sex, but I am sure I was typical of my generation in not being aware of all its possible permutations. Nor was a generous interlarding of Anglo-Saxon words, a number of which were regarded as too basic for a standard dictionary, ever a feature of open conversation, but they were all present in this one. I remember I listened to the first few sallies with horror. Then the whole thing struck me as being incredibly funny. I shook with laughter underneath blankets and when the noise had died down went unconcernedly to sleep.

Somewhere around the middle of May 1940, when I had been in the Army about two months, the unit suddenly moved. We were taken over to Lavenham and put into a former weaving shed, a dry cosy place after the draughty horse-hair factory. At the end of the long room some of the looms remained, with the ends of cloth on them, just as they had been left when the last weaver departed, how many years before?

The next day we were introduced for the first time to the lorries of the unit. Apart from the stores' trucks, the unit was remarkably ill-equipped, for the lorries we were now invited to clean and so get acquainted with seemed to be relics of the First World War. They were great high Scammells with two sets of wheels at the back and canvas 'tilts' overall. The strangest thing to me was that they had no windscreens, only a canvas apron which presumably in bad weather the driver and his mate tied round their necks.

We had scarcely sampled the fleshpots of Newbiggin – the fleshpots being represented by some of the best fish and chips I have ever eaten, cooked by two old ladies in a poky kitchen over a coal-fuelled stove – when I and all my group of fellow conscripts were suddenly and precipitately dispatched by rail nearly all the way back to where we had just come from. Our new place of residence was Norwich. The next morning we were escorted across the town to the motor works of Messrs Mann Egerton near the castle, where we learned we were to be put through a ten week course as motor mechanics. Whether we had any aptitude for or an inclination towards engineering had not been enquired of, but so far as I was concerned, I welcomed the opportunity of at last learning something useful.

The opening of the course contained a feature we had not previously been granted: a 'welcome' and a 'pep-talk'. The German *blitzkrieg* on Belgium and France had started by now, which gave point to what was said. The instructors were all civilian, and very good they were too. We worked in well-equipped workshops and lecture rooms with a wealth of cut-away models of vehicle parts and real engines to take to pieces.

The food, including meat, and to a lesser extent the vegetables, was appalling. Of the poorest quality from the start, being mainly fat and gristle, the meat had been cooked, sliced and re-heated, and was swimming in grease. In this barracks the orderly officer came round with the traditional question of 'Any complaints?' Some of the hardier souls spoke up, with the murmured support of us more timid folk. But the cookhouse knew how to deal with this – they had obviously met it before. The word was passed round that if further complaints were made we should be forced to parade before meals. This would have been a most inconvenient imposition. Luckily, we did not need to go there very often: when we did, most of the food went into the swill bins.

So the course came to an end and we were despatched to Newbiggin again. We were not very surprised, having begun to know the Army by this time, that the unit was no longer there. Security now having become quite tight, it took the rail transport officer some time to find out where we should be sent to join it.

Chapter 2

Training – North of England

The company was now under canvas in part of a stately home which I think was Mitford, the ancestral seat of the Redesdale family, to the west of Morpeth. In our absence it had been equipped with some modern lorries, the 3-ton Bedfords with square bonnets which became standard to the Army from that time on. There was a more business-like aspect to the company as a result. Perhaps the capitulation of France on 22 June was giving a hint of urgency.

It might have been thought that having sent us on a long and expensive course, the Army would have found scope for our new-found skills. Such was not the case. The lorries were too precious to be touched, except for cleaning, by semi-skilled hands. Apart from the usual chores around the camp I remember doing nothing except making camouflage nets, the use of which had become an obsession. They had to be put over the lorries whenever they stopped, even if the effect was to make them look like bushes in the middle of city streets.

It can have been scarcely two or three weeks after our return when the unit moved again. Our destination this time was Belsay, an estate about a dozen miles north-west of Newcastle, and so not very far away from Mitford. In an article in *The Times* of 22 September 1972 is the following description:

> The 35-bedroom Belsay Hall is in the style of a Greek temple rising above landscaped gardens and built in a honey-coloured stone quarried on the estate. Along its front it has a row of Doric pilasters with, on either side of the main entrance, two mighty Doric columns.

The Hall was built in 1810–17, but in the grounds and peeping over the trees like the Sleeping Beauty's fairy castle was the fourteenth-century Belsay Castle, which seemed to me to be as authentic and genuine a medieval castle as one could wish for, with no later improvements or restorations. The grounds around the Hall were extensive. Many of the trees

21

were firs and there were thick shrubberies enclosing or bordering the several roads and lanes which ran through the estate. This dark foliage, combined with the brooding appearance of the Hall itself, gave the whole place an air of great melancholy as if there had never been sun and laughter there. It was said that two previous owners had committed suicide. If they had, it was understandable.

The company was now, I suppose (for we were never informed of it), on active service. The division was deployed to resist invasion on the Northumbrian coast, the remoteness of which did not reflect highly on the confidence placed in the division. It was our function to supply ammunition to the infantry and artillery units, and gradually dumps of shells and small-arms ammunition were formed under the trees. This was of course the post-Dunkirk period when the Army found itself short of many of its essential supplies and those it had were concentrated in likely invasion areas in the south. In our distant sector some of the guns on the coast were of obsolete pattern – such things as 6-pounders, 12-pounders and 18-pounders – and for these there existed perhaps as few as a dozen rounds of ammunition. When these had been fired off the gun would have been useless for ever more. I recall looking at some wooden ammo boxes which were noticeable for being splintered and broken. They were long and narrow and it took me a minute or two to understand why they had 'US Army Expeditionary Force, France' (or some similar legend) stencilled on the side. These were shells left over from the First World War – ammunition for the famous French 75s. Some work was done repairing their crates but one day they were suddenly taken away – condemned as dangerous.

Apart from the Bedford lorries, the company had acquired a number of civilian vehicles, presumably by requisition. These were some of the most clapped-out old wrecks I have ever seen. After extensive work upon them and a short period of service, they then disappeared, greatly improved and raised in value, to their original owners.

The skill most highly prized in the unit was that of driving. The lorries were cumbersome things with difficult gearboxes, and having demonstrated my incompetence, including putting one in a ditch (happily without damage), I was rarely asked to drive. No one was given any tuition in what was, after all, a central requirement in a transport unit.

Of modern weapons at this time we saw very little. Indeed for a time we even had no rifles and those that replaced them later were of a Canadian type. We were given instruction on how to use the Lewis-gun, a light machine gun from the First World War which had a circular magazine on top. It was liable to jam but was supposed to be effective against aircraft.

Another weapon of which the unit had one example was the Boyes anti-tank gun, a long-barrelled oversized rifle with a bipod support, discharging a .500 bullet.[1] How this could be effective against a German tank I could never imagine. Later we handled 2-pounder anti-tank shells which were supposed to be better. In this connection it struck me then, and it strikes me now, how different was the British military terminology from the German. We would talk of an anti-tank gun; they of a tank-hunter. A weapon which came my way later was called the Projector Infantry Anti-Tank (PIAT); the German equivalent was the 'Mailed Fist'. If a prize were to be offered for the most uninspiring piece of Army nomenclature it would surely be won by PAD (or Passive Air Defence). PAD was largely concerned with precautions against aerial gas attack and one could gather from the frequency of the drills that this possibility was very much feared. We had been provided with a service gas mask which hung in a canvas case on our chests and a 'gas cape', a garment of camouflaged oil-skin which was carried in a roll above our back pack. This to my mind gave us the look of French soldiers on the retreat from Moscow.

On the word 'gas', or on the ringing of the 'gas alarm', which was the steel rim of a lorry wheel hung up with a striker, one rapidly donned a gas mask and released the rolled gas cape by tugging a cord. It enveloped you, pulling the hood over your head and around your face. The ensemble was then completed by the inverted dish of the steel helmet on top. We would thus in theory be protected from the 'rain of deadly dew'. Efforts were made to familiarise us with working in gas masks by requiring every activity to be done in them for one hour per week. They were hot, smelly, uncomfortable and very limiting.

A further drill was intended to be a protection against enemy aircraft, with us standing with our rifles in serried ranks, out in the open. Someone shouted 'aircraft right' or 'aircraft left' (as though our senses of sight and hearing had left us), whereupon the whole body of men turned and clicked their triggers towards the sky. We were told this was effective against ground-strafing aeroplanes. What the aeroplanes would have thought of it, I really cannot imagine.

A major feature of life at Belsay was guard duty. I suppose in the prevailing climate of anxiety, which emphasised and indeed over-emphasised the danger from fifth-columnists and spies, let alone actual invasion, matters had been greatly tightened up since the spring. The result was that the Hall was nothing if not well guarded day and night.

There was one significant night when I was on sentry duty at the main gate. This was on Saturday, 7 September 1940. Somebody bustled into the guard tent saying that the invasion had started and reinforced this piece of news with an issue of live rifle ammunition – the first time we had ever been entrusted with any. We learnt later that this was in response to the code message 'Cromwell', meaning 'invasion imminent', which had been circulated to Southern Command and had led to the Home Guard in some places ringing the church bells. Other commands were given the warning 'for information only', but ours acted on it. That the Germans held invasion exercises is true, but what sparked off the alert I never found out. My drunken comrades coming up the road from their Saturday night out did not take it seriously.

We were at Belsay for six months or more, which included my first week's leave in October, Christmas and some extremely heavy snow. On Christmas Day there was a general relaxation and a special dinner. The dinner was a good one, held inside the Hall and, in accordance with tradition, we common soldiers were served by the officers and sergeants. The officer commanding brought round the beer in a white enamelled bathroom jug. The occasion was a little marred for me, and perhaps for others, by a tactless speech by the sergeant major in which he congratulated the unit for being composed of volunteers, all but a negligible few. This did nothing for my sense of oneness with it.[2]

The nearest cinema was at Newcastle and we could get passes to go down there at weekends. Sometimes the unit would transport us in a 'passion waggon' – a lorry laid on to get us back at midnight. One of the men called up at the same time as I, had his home in Sunderland and he sometimes used to take me with him for a sample of northern hospitality. Considering the circumstances of wartime the family were most kind. In civilian life this man was an unskilled factory worker living in Hitchin. He had been brought down there, I believe, by a government scheme designed to give employment to people from 'depressed areas'. We remade contact after the war, but the meeting was not a success. I always regretted this and that I was unable to repay his hospitality in some way. But Army friendships stem largely from a common need in exceptional circumstances and whilst they might conceivably continue on a man-to-man basis afterwards, they rarely survive contrasting backgrounds of work, family and (let's face it) social class.

Our main recreation had necessarily to be in camp. The Nissen Hut billet (these were sheds made of great curved sheets of corrugated iron which were bolted together to form a tunnel-like compartment, the ends closed in by wooden walls with two windows and a door) had electric light and an iron 'tortoise' stove, which, fed by coal and logs, could be heated up to keep the place very comfortable even in winter. This was our home and the roof over our personal possessions.

It was a convention that one's bedspace was exclusive to oneself and another only entered it by permission. Here we cleaned brass, blanco'd webbing equipment, talked intermittently, read paperback books, wrote letters and listened to the radio. The radio had been the gift of some welfare organisation and for some reason was held to be in my custody. By mischance its glass dial plate had been broken but as we adhered to the 'light' programme (or its then equivalent) this mattered not at all. In those days portable radios had to have both dry batteries and a wet 'accumulator' and it was always a problem to keep the latter adequately charged. We used to get workshops to do it.

Our main listening was the news, but the popular comedy programmes such as 'It's That Man Again' and 'Much Binding in the Marsh' had a regular following so far as guard duties and exercises allowed. But of all the memories of those days it is the voice of Vera Lynn singing 'We'll Meet Again' and 'There'll be Blue Birds over the White Cliffs of Dover' that remains most vividly with me. Sentimental yes, but a sentimentality perhaps understandable only by those who know what it is to be compulsorily removed from a life with love to a life without love, from a life of security and comfort to one of insecurity and discomfort, and enduring a separation which might, indeed did, go on for years and facing a future which was to contain we knew not what, or which might not be a future at all.

But the main recreation was the NAAFI, a gaunt bare room with a plank table across one end where men exempted from military service (on the grounds it was believed, probably correctly, that they were homosexuals) sold bottled beer in any desired quantity. To the consumption of this we talked, laughed and sang songs, until the time came to stagger back to the billet, rarely drunk but often 'under the influence', to turn into our blanket beds (thoughtfully made up in advance) sedated against the weather, the Army and the rigours of life generally.

This may be an appropriate place to say something about the ever-interesting topic of sex. As Kipling said, 'Why, single men in barracks don't grow into plaster saints.' It is also recognised that Mars and Venus go hand in hand. There is no doubt that in the Army there was a high consciousness of sex and much talk about it, though this was always jocular, mostly bawdy and never serious. Many words with sexual meanings were transposed to become ordinary substantives and other parts of speech. This could lead to unfortunate lapses during our rare re-entries into civilian life, as when one of my friends, a very respectable type, whilst at the family tea-table, asked someone to 'pass the f **king butter'. This was the terrible, the totally obscene word, and as he told me, his father just leant across, smacked him around the head and said nothing.

But as to the prevalence of sexual activity, it is difficult to tell. Certainly there was the conventional assumption that when the men went into Newcastle they went for one purpose only, and much ragging and jesting, with a little boasting, went on about that. But it takes two to make a situation and many men did not go out with girls. Indeed, such was the noted absence of libido in many that some believed their inclinations were officially damped by 'something in the porridge', but I don't know if there was any truth in this. However, it was clear that sexual mores were a matter of class. At that time the middle-class ethic was definitely chastity (in the sense of technically remaining a virgin) before marriage and fidelity within it. Nice girls just didn't or were not supposed to. By the end of the war this had changed, the Americans having a hand in doing the changing.

In 1940, however, the working class had a different attitude. Casual sex was apparently quite customary with them and very little was with prostitutes. It was mainly a case of the girl willingly allowing, even expecting, the evening to be rounded off by sexual intercourse as part of her contribution to the occasion. This was done purely on the basis of liking; only the middle class required the fact or fiction of love to be necessary.[3]

The amount of sexual encounters which had been going on was, however, illustrated, even in those early days, by official worry over the spread of venereal disease. At Belsay we were one day summoned to a lecture by the medical officer which was all about VD, how it was caught and what to do about it. We were enjoined to wash the part most at risk as soon as possible after connection and disinfect it with toothpaste. This meeting

26

was the first serious discussion of sex I had ever heard, apart from that among friends. One man fainted during it. Soon afterwards, a system of early treatment (ET) centres was instituted. This was a room or tent set apart for those who had succumbed to temptation, to visit on returning from the adventure. It provided an 'ET kit' which included a tube of ointment with a syringe-type nozzle. Whether condoms were ever issued I do not know. Possibly they could be also obtained there.

I was never aware of anyone becoming infected with VD, although at various times during the war it became, I believe, a threat to the efficiency of the Army. Nor, at this stage, do I think there was any homosexuality in the unit, though statistically there must have been homosexuals among us. Perhaps to be so inclined openly was a crime as it was in the Navy. By us it was not regarded with horror, only as an unfortunate eccentricity. The men behind the NAAFI bar never mixed with the soldiers. They were never seen around in this close-knit community. Where they lived or where they went, no one knew. I have often wondered if this was deliberate policy to prevent us from being 'contaminated'.

One day it was announced that the major (an Olympian figure to us) would carry out an inspection. Tool kits were laid out on the lorries' tailboards. When he came to me his eyes bored into mine in the way officers were trained to look at the rank and file, and he declared (having found nothing wrong with my turn-out) that he could tell at once that a vehicle was properly maintained simply by looking at the tool kit. If that was in order, everything was in order. This vapid assertion was matched later in my experience of General Browning, who declared, in a leaflet issued to airborne troops, that he could judge a unit's efficiency by the alacrity with which its men saluted his car.

It was during our time at Belsay that someone must have thought I ought to be given a proper job, for I was required to take a 'trade test' of the skills I was assumed to have acquired at Norwich months previously. As a result I was reclassified from 'driver' to 'motor mechanic'. Though I could not have known it at the time, the trade classification had an effect on my later history, as will be described. It probably too stopped me being sent on a draft to Africa or Singapore, as many of my comrades were during 1941, as possibly enough motor mechanics had been selected already.

Chapter 3

Training – South of England

As winter came to an end, so did our stay in the North Country. In the spring we moved to the area of Stow-in-the-Wold. My part of the company were settled in farm buildings at Lower Swell, a mile or so down the hill. I remember particularly that springtime because a flock of ewes in a field near us were lambing: unfortunately there was something wrong – they had been tupped by an errant ram and were too immature to drop their young. Consequently, they just died of exhaustion where they were. I never saw anyone tending them or giving them a thought.

Scenically there could have been no better place to be at that time. The weather was fine, the air pellucid, and the local names – Bourton-on-the-Water, Upper Slaughter, the Windrush – real poetry. We slept in double-decker bunks in well-built stables: 'These are meant for horses, you know,' said the visiting general. 'See you look after them!' Our mess-room was a wooden hut in the farmyard, the guardroom a tack-room which somehow got set alight, destroying some valuable harness. I have to confess that I enjoyed those summer months. They were almost paradise after the gloom of Belsay. The character of the company had greatly changed for the better. It had received several drafts of men, some regular soldiers who had been at Dunkirk ('Dunkirk heroes' they were unkindly labelled), and several drafts of National Service intake from a depot at Nottingham. What the CSM thought of this dilution of the pure strain of volunteers I do not know but there was a wider and more interesting range of talent than the unit had had before.[1]

We did very few drills and only a little training, mainly I suppose because we were considered to be through all that. We were introduced to the Bren gun by a Regular Army sergeant who confirmed my view that if a regular was a good type, he was a really good type, the opposite also being the case. The Bren also gave the officers some innocent fun in requiring us to dig a gun-pit in a field and go through the motions of combating enemy aircraft, in the event of enemy aircraft having taken it into their heads to

29

shoot up an obscure formation in a field at Lower Swell, Oxfordshire. So work did not loom very large. Some of us even played tennis at the local big-wig's house and I was befriended by some middle-aged ladies who lived on the farm and fed me with delicious salads. We had greater freedom than at Belsay, and could go to the local pub, the Golden Ball, or up the hill to Stow-on-the-Wold whenever we were off duty. It was here that I took a risk which, in retrospect, was one of several during my Army days, the stupidity of which I have since marvelled at.

On one of my 'leaves' I had returned to the unit on my own motor-cycle. Petrol was of course strictly rationed and could be obtained legally only on the production of coupons which for 'non-essential users' were very few. The lorries were full of petrol: what more natural than that they should be made to yield up small quantities for my private use? (In self-defence I ought perhaps to add that by the moral standards of wartime, and particularly those of the Army, there was nothing wrong in doing this – provided of course that one was not found out.) Any criminal act needs both temptation and opportunity, and I had plenty of both. I only needed to be on guard duty during the hours of darkness and a piece of rubber tubing and a petrol can did the rest.

What was idiotic about this was that the petrol was not the same as that obtained in a lawful manner. It contained an easily identifiable green dye. The fact that I had my motor-cycle with me was generally known. Had anyone decided to concern himself with the matter I would have been charged, court-martialled and sent 'over the wall' into a military prison for at least six months. One of my comrades had so offended and had been punished: the experience had been so grim that one could never get out of him what it had been like. Another man sentenced to a similar period for a cheque fraud came back looking like a ghost. However, I was never brought to account.

For the war was not going well. Ever since Dunkirk a year and a half back, our country had stood alone facing across the narrow waters of the Channel a victorious, ruthless and apparently unstoppable enemy. In May 1941 our last foothold on the continent of Europe had been lost with the bloody defeats of our troops in Greece and Crete. The main theatre of war against the Axis was North Africa, where, after some spectacular successes against the Italians, our Army was now facing the German Afrika Korps under Rommel, with such lack of effectiveness that by January 1942 the enemy stood at the frontiers of Egypt and there seemed nothing to stop him from advancing to Suez – the lifeline to India, Australia and New Zealand, upon whose reinforcement we were heavily dependent – and taking over the whole of the Middle East. In December 1941 the Japanese swept through our possessions in the Far East in episodes of quite unbelievable cruelty intended to humiliate before the rest of the world our once great Empire. They sank, by aerial bombing, the vast capital ships HMS *Repulse* and HMS *Prince of Wales* off Malaya, a major defeat for the hitherto successful Royal Navy, whilst with the fall in February 1942 of the major fortress of Singapore came the greatest military disaster ever to be inflicted on the British Army. There was not much to show for the two years of blackout, air-raids, ever more stringent rationing and the total disruption of so many lives.

Even the two events which really held the seeds of victory were at that time not giving much reason for hope. Hitler had invaded Russia in June 1941, thus taking on the enormous manpower of that vast country, and by November the Germans were at the gates of Moscow. The Japanese by their attack on Pearl Harbor in December 1941 had brought the immense industrial potential, as well as the eventually doughty fighting strength, of the United States into the conflict, but had destroyed the latter's Pacific fleet in what was intended to be a knock-out blow. All was much in the balance with the scales weighted on the enemies' side.

The national mood was very sombre. For myself, an insignificant participant in the world-wide convulsion, I had my own reason to feel despondent. I had now been in the Army for getting on for two years; I had found no useful job to do in it; I had hardly done a single useful day's work. In itself this was of no importance. I had seen in the RASC no great desire to get on with the war, and it was clear to me that if it was to be won someone would have to get on with it. My younger brother had been captured at Singapore, whilst I was underemployed, well-fed and within reach of home. I was ashamed of my own lack of progress and disgusted with the Army's indolence and lack of any sense of urgency at a time when the country's survival seemed at stake. What I did not know was, for me and for it, that was all to change.

In the late summer, in 1941, we were moved to Stoke Poges, just north of Slough, Buckinghamshire. Many a time I have driven along the road where it turns left to Gerrards Cross, and remembered how I used to guard the gate of the large house there. Later I was sent to workshops again a mile or so away at Framewood Manor. Here things began to fall apart. All of a sudden, drafts of men were sent on embarkation leave. Some ended up in Africa, among them a friend of mine who sought me out in Italy nearly two years later, as will be recounted; others were sent out to reinforce failure in the Far East, many never to return. Among these were some of the young men with whom I had waited for the lorry at Sudbury railway station.

Chapter 4

'Total Soldiers'

To explain what happened next I must backtrack a little ... As I have already indicated, I did not like the Army – or at least what I had seen of it in the 54th Divisional Ammunition Company, RASC – and I had no reason to believe that the Army liked me. It was clear that I was a misfit. I could, moreover, perceive no place where such talents as I had, if any, could be put to proper use. It was not surprising therefore that, probably at Lower Swell, there had appeared in company orders an invitation to those who desired to do so to apply for flying duties in the RAF. I was among those who put their names forward.

This was not the first time I had considered the possibility of becoming an aviator. In the months before the war, during the period when it had become generally apparent that war was inevitable (which can be dated from the Nazi invasion of Czechoslovakia in the spring of 1939), I had made enquiries about the Civil Air Guard, a sort of Territorial Army of aircrew, of which there was a unit at Luton Airport, not far from Hitchin. I had even gone so far as to have a medical check with my doctor to establish whether I was fit enough. However, the library was so short of staff that I was unable to have Saturday afternoons off for training, so I did nothing more about it.

In the Army, as will have already been apparent, one was never told anything and one never expected anything. It was a surprise therefore when quite soon I was summoned to attend for selection procedure at RAF Cardington, near Bedford. We were put through medical and physical checks, blowing columns of mercury up tubes, and I seem to remember being swung around in a chair. Colour sense was tested by means of a book with multicoloured patterns on the pages; I was told that a surprising number of men failed in this. We were also given a written intelligence test. It had been understood that this would take place next morning and that we were free till then. Returning later to our billet, we found that some of the men who had stayed in had already been given the test. This

33

was fortunate: they told us what the questions were, and surprisingly the same questions were put before us the next morning. I and others were advised we had passed and would be notified.

I now began to see new vistas opening before me. I bought a book on air navigation (because I saw myself – I don't know why – in that branch of the service rather than as a pilot) and it was the topic which became my major interest during the period of excused duties which I was given whilst nursing a damaged finger. In spirit I had already detached myself. Nothing happened, however. Weeks went past and still nothing happened. In the autumn, when the company moved to Suffolk, I had still not been called into the RAF. It became obvious that I never would be.

It was not until well after the war that somehow I got to know the background to this. Since the beginning the RAF had been the only one of the three services which had been in a position to carry the offensive into the heart of the enemy's territory, and the loss of aircrew had been great. The Army had been seen to contain a large number of fit and under-employed people, craving a useful job. Given the chance, volunteers came forward in large numbers and some I believe were transferred. Then the Army woke up to the fact that they were in danger of losing a large element of their more intelligent people and had the scheme closed down. At the same time the idea that the Army itself needed an airborne element in addition to the paratroops, the first unit of which appeared in 1940, began to gather momentum. In the course of this, gliders came on the scene and gliders needed people to fly them. The Glider Pilot Regiment (GPR) was first formed in January 1942.

I have no clear recollection of where and when I heard of the Regiment. It was probably early in 1942 or more likely autumn/winter 1941 when we were in the mill at Beyton and thus about four or five months after I had been passed for aircrew duties. My memory is that somehow orders came down from above that those who had been selected for the RAF should be given the opportunity to volunteer. Without much reflection I did so.

So, one fine morning I found myself setting out in full marching order with everything I possessed. No one bade me farewell, not I believe out of malice but because they confidently expected me to be back very shortly. In another section I had come across a man who had in fact achieved transfer to the GPR some months earlier but had not made the grade. He was full of complaints about the 'bullshit', i.e. the drills and spit and polish, he had found there. Members of special forces, it transpired, were not permanently transferred; you still belonged to where you came from. Hence the risk of 'RTU' (Returned to Unit) being stamped on one's papers was an ever-present one.

I reported to the Regiment on 10 August 1942. On passing through London I took the opportunity of calling on my father, who was on the staff of the *Financial Times* in Coleman Street.

Two things left the train at Lavington station on the edge of Salisbury Plain: myself and a coffin. At first I thought the latter was for an unlucky glider pilot but soon found that no flying training was done at the place I was going to. I had little knowledge of and no personal acquaintance with gliders. I had known of course that the Germans had used them with great effect in the invasions of Belgium and Holland in 1940. What I did not know was that their airborne invasion of Crete in May 1941 had been so costly in lives and equipment that they never used gliders in an assault role again. The only glider flying I had ever seen was at Dunstable and that was not gliding but sailplaning.

A truck summoned from the station took me to Tilshead Camp, the Regiment's then base, where I reported to the orderly room. Here it was at once apparent that I was in a different sort of Army. There was a neatness about the room and a smartness about its occupants that I had never met before, even though the latter were clothed in identically the same manner as I was. They wore, however, the maroon-coloured beret with the silver badge of the Army Air Corps, not the demeaning forage cap.

A soldier at a desk looked at me appraisingly but without the 'look what the dog's brought in' expression, which superior ranks in the RASC used to cultivate in relations with their inferiors. He was an obviously very fit young man, scarcely older than myself, in well-pressed shirt-sleeves. It came as a shock to realise he was wearing a sergeant major's crown on a band on his wrist; sergeant majors in my experience had been old sweats, rather past it. After a few preliminaries he said, nodding towards the gas-mask case hanging on my chest, 'I should get rid of that, if I were you.' The 'that' was the unsightly sack of a sandbag in which we had been required to envelop the gas-mask case. I soon got the message: nothing second-rate was tolerated in this outfit.

I was assigned to a hut among the new intake, most of whom had been there a few days already. From every branch of the Army, infantry, signals, artillery, engineers, and from all four parts of the United Kingdom, they all carried the badges and some the characteristic headgear of their own units. Lance corporals and corporals retained their rank; sergeants, we found later, were also among us but had their separate accommodation.

We fed well; there were papers and magazines to read; and that week-end a lecture had been arranged to be given by some MP or 'official spokesman' regarding some aspect of the international situation. Great heavens, we were assumed to have interests beyond women and beer! The distinguished lecturer was plied with probing questions by people of all ranks or of no rank at all, and they were speaking out in the presence of senior officers who were actually listening to what they said! This was something new. I learnt later that this was all part of the training. The Regiment had been founded by Colonel Rock, a well-liked engineer officer who was one of those present at the lecture. Unhappily he was soon after killed whilst training in night flying. His next-in-command, Major, later Colonel, later Brigadier George Chatterton then took over and brought a dynamism, if not fanaticism, to bear on his task.

Chatterton wanted to produce the 'Total Soldier': we were to fly every-thing that flew, shoot everything that shot, drive everything that drove, etc., etc. (To this litany there was an additional area of omnicompetence added by my more earthy colleagues.) To what extent he succeeded may appear later. The very highest standards were demanded from us from the start. The 'bullshit' my former comrade had complained of was the insistence on the smartest possible turnout, enforced by close but, oddly, not hostile inspection parades every morning. Clothes and equipment had to be spotless (we used to sleep on our trousers to get a good crease), everything which could be blanco'd was blanco'd, the brass shone. I never heard any resentment about this, an obvious test of morale. It was rather nice to be looking and feeling on top of the world after so long feeling one was at the bottom of it.

If any piece of equipment was worn or below standard it could be replaced at once and without question at the quartermaster's stores. The QM himself took an interest in seeing that our uniform fitted properly, another revelation. After the morning parade we had an hour's 'square-bashing', foot-drill to begin with and rifle drill later. Of course, we all knew the basics, but each regiment and service did things at their own tempo and a norm had to be achieved. For this purpose two sergeant majors had been imported, one from the Irish Guards and the other from the Coldstream Guards, both redoubtable on parade but genial off it. If I say that we reached a very high standard in a very short time I hope

I am not being self-congratulatory, but I have often seen drill since by regular soldiers which was nothing to ours. For my part I enjoyed it – there is nothing like knowing one is doing something really well. We drilled and marched at the pace of the Brigade of Guards, that is relatively slowly. In the end we could go through a cycle of drill movements in perfect time without a command being given.

Physical activity was complemented by mental activity. We had sessions on map-reading, aircraft identification and the Morse code. I think we did some shooting and learned to fire the Sten gun, then a new weapon, at this time. As I have already said I was always a good shot. One instructor offered a prize to anyone who could get more hits on a target, firing from the hip, than he could. I certainly beat him but got no prize: he said the target had had bullet holes on it already.

We had no inkling of it at the time but our base at Tilshead was the base from which the Bruneval raid, one of the attacks on German installations on the coast of France, had been launched earlier that year. We might have been rubbing shoulders with people who had taken part in that and similar cloak-and-dagger activities.

Chapter 5

Flying at Last

The general assumption was that we would be at Tilshead for a month or more. In the event (and I find it very surprising in retrospect, but my flying log book confirms it) all that I have described was contained within ten days, at the end of which we were 'made up' to corporals and told that our flying training was to begin. We were whisked off to Derbyshire at short notice. The date was 20 August 1942.

Our base was Burnaston, near Derby. It had been, I believe, a privately owned airfield before the war which the RAF had taken over and developed as an Elementary Flying Training School (EFTS). It was here that pilots-in-the-making were given the basic instruction both in the air and on the ground which would fit them for 'conversion' later to operational aircraft, in our case gliders. To begin with, however, we did not sleep on the airfield but in the dormitories at Repton College, from which we were taken daily by coaches driven by the Woman's Auxiliary Air Force (WAAF).

The earliest part of our training also did not take place at Burnaston itself, but at a small airfield at Abbots Bromley a few miles away. One day whilst travelling to it we saw men weirdly dressed and carrying the stags' antlers which are part of the age-old festival held there. It was at Abbots Bromley that we first sat in the cockpit of a de Havilland Tiger Moth and were given 'air experience'.

The Tiger Moth (DH82) was a small canvas and metal biplane in which the instructor sat in the front cockpit just aft of and below the upper wing whilst the pupil sat behind. Communication between the two was by voice tube which led from a mouthpiece in one cockpit to earphones inserted into the close-fitting leather flying helmet which both instructor and pupil wore. It was of course cold up in the sky in an open cockpit. The flying helmet came well down on the forehead and was strapped beneath the chin and, the upper part of the face being covered by large goggles, only part of it sensed the icy air. The rest of our body, over our normal battledress, was encased firstly in a thin silky one-piece garment which zipped up the front and then a 'Sidcot Suit', a sort of gabardine boiler suit with fur collar and cuffs. Our hands had a three-fold covering of a pair of silk gloves, a pair of camel-hair gloves, and a large pair of fleece-lined leather gauntlets over all. This was of course the maximum protection provided and we so enveloped ourselves only when the weather was really cold. Usually, we would restrict ourselves to the Sidcot Suit and gauntlets, which over our uniform was quite sufficient.

For our feet, the greatest joy of all, we wore calf-length sheepskin flying-boots. The boots were marks of our trade and when travelling by rail some of the men, most surprisingly, often could find no room for them in their kitbags and carried them dangling from their shoulders, to the hoped-for admiration of all the world. The ambition of some was to bribe or trick stores into letting them have a pair for the girlfriend – an ambition not easily realised as they were expensive items. Thus garbed and with a parachute pack strapped to shoulders waist and crutch, we were put through our initial sequence of training.

The objective at this stage was the 'first solo', a milestone not only in flying training but also in life, because it is indeed one of the unique experiences. Each of us had been assigned to an instructor, and I fell to the lot of one whom I shall designate Flying Officer D. By my standards he was an old man and he certainly wore medal ribbons which seemed to date from the First World War. He was both Scottish and cantankerous, and his instruction was so exacting that, apart from an undoubted slow-ness of uptake in this strange environment, I began to get demoralised and feel, as he did, that I would never make the grade. On one occasion he roared down the voice tube in his heavy accent: 'Eshby, ye're a fool: ye climb at 55, and one day ye'll climb at 55, and ye'll stall and ye'll cra-ash, and ye'll die-e-e.' That was enough to encourage anyone.

I was now friendly with a man named Peter and, on exchanging impres-sions, I found he was having a different experience altogether. He had been assigned to an American pilot, 'Tex' Parker, who was one of those gentle-men adventurers who had come over before the USA had entered the war and had been formed by the RAF into the Eagle Squadron. Trainee pilots were allowed twelve hours flying time before they went solo, and if they did not achieve this in the time they were washed out. I had already clocked up eight hours and was getting nowhere. I approached the flight lieutenant in charge (RAF officers, especially the flying types, were easily approachable compared with their Army counterparts) and I asked to be transferred to Tex. The flight lieutenant understood – I got a feeling he had had similar requests from Flying Officer D's pupils before – and arranged the transfer.

I had no trepidation about becoming the sole master of my fate and taking off, flying and landing an aircraft reliant absolutely on my own skill and beyond help from anyone else, which is the essence of the experience. I just had a not un-enjoyable frisson of excitement. The first sensation was taxiing round the field to the down-wind end, finding it a little strange to have an empty cockpit in front for the first time. One turned the aircraft across wind, did a rapid check of instruments and controls, and waited for the green flash of the Aldis light. That given, one turned towards the sausage-like wind-sock, slowly but steadily opened the throttle until, with the little craft bumping and bouncing on the turf, one had enough speed to push the nose down to get the tail up. The far hedge seemed to be getting remarkable near. Then with the flicker of an eye at the air-speed indicator, one pulled the stick back, the bumping ceased, the hedge went underneath, the world fell away, and there ahead, beyond an ever-widening landscape, was a remote horizon upon which one levelled out and set the nose of the plane. Throttling back to a steady purr, it was possible to set the trimmers so that the plane assumed a steady balance – this was the secret: one did not so much fly the plane as help it to fly – and one had a few minutes in which one could sit comfortably and have a look round. For some reason I thought of my brother John and wondered what he would think if he knew I was up there. Then it was time to think of coming down.

All the pieces of the chequer-board fields looked alike and I did not immediately identify the airfield, but there it was, a tiny patch with toy-like sheds and aeroplanes. I had done the prescribed circuit and now began to sink lower and lower at the correct place and height turning into wind. Everything now began to get larger and larger and pass underneath faster and faster, until the moment came to pull the nose up and put the tail down and let the plane sink to the ground on its wheels and skid. Then the moment of taxiing back to the watch-office. I had done it, I could fly, I was henceforth set apart from other men. When I asked the flight lieutenant how it had looked, 'Landing a bit wheely' was all he said.

Readers of the present and future under whose eyes this memoir will come may well feel that there was something naive and vainglorious about my euphoria on achieving my first solo. This is understandable in an era in which flying has become more commonplace than travelling by train. They should reflect, however, how different things were at the time of which I write. Although commercial routes were gradually criss-crossing the world in the thirties, their use was restricted to the very few. Flying was still regarded as hazardous and there was a considerable mystique about it. Very few people had ever been up in a plane, even as passengers. It so happened that I was one of that very few, for not only had I made a short trip in Germany in 1934 but with my brother John I had also, for the fun of it, done the return flight over the Solent from the Isle of Wight to Portsmouth. But no one else among all my relatives and acquaintances had ever been off the ground. It will be recalled that even the prime minister, Neville Chamberlain, flew for the first time in his life when he visited Hitler in Germany in 1938, and that was regarded as a wonderful achievement, particularly for a man of his age.

If merely going up in a plane was glamorous, how much more so was the ability to fly one. Pilots were thought to have exceptional qualities. People paid to watch public shows like the Hendon Air Pageant or Sir Alan Cobham's Flying Circus, the very name of the latter having overtones of dare-devilry. Among ourselves we used to refer to flying as 'dicing' – dicing with death.

There followed three months of continuous instruction and practice flying at the main airfield at Burnaston, together with sessions in the classroom and in the link trainer. Having become proficient on the Tiger Moth, we were introduced to the Miles Magister, a low-wing monoplane of a more up-to-date design but of a less tractable nature, and our training from now on alternated between these two types.

The best trips were when we were sent off to do aerobatics. One climbed to about 7,000ft and threw the plane about at will. The Tiger Moth was a steady old kite with 'slots' or auxiliary aerofoils on the wings to give added lift, and for aerobatics one closed these which made the plane much more lively. Looping the loop, which looks one of the most spectacular manoeuvres, was comparatively easy.

Towards the end of the course we were put onto night flying, in the course of which I had a little adventure which might have ended in disaster had I not been well trained in blind flying. It was a damp misty November night with no moon. In those days the flare path was just what its name implies – a single line of flickering tongues of flame from containers which

42

were very like oil-filled watering-cans with a wick in the spout. There was no horizon, nothing but a misty blackness, so that, after taking one's direction from the flares, one headed off into the murk dependent on instruments alone. There was no radio communication, indeed no communication at all save by lamp from the ground, in those days. Now the magnetic compass is at best an imperfect instrument, especially in a light plane. The needle has an 'angle of dip' which places its centre of gravity behind the pivot. Thus, if the plane does a flat turn the centre of gravity swings around the pivot and the needle points anywhere but to the North.

On leaving the flare-path one was supposed to level out at a certain height for a minute or two, when one would find oneself over a line of 'leading out lights' positioned in a field. On this flight, after the prescribed time had elapsed, they were nowhere to be seen. I was up there by myself in complete darkness except for the dim glow of the instruments, not knowing where I was and with no celestial or terrestrial object visible from which I could get my bearings. It was then, and is now, my firm opinion that more lives are lost by panic than by anything else. I remember making a conscious decision not to panic. Using the artificial horizon, I levelled off and set myself to fly the course set on the compass and to give myself a minute or two to think things out. I concluded that I had veered off to the left after leaving the airfield and that the compass had swung as I had turned. I therefore presumed that I was well ahead of the flare-path but on a course parallel to it.

I decided to fly square courses of so many minutes on one bearing followed by the same number on another at right angles. It was lonely up there in pitch darkness, completely beyond all human aid. At one stage I let off some flares which for night flying were hung under the wings, to see if I could see anything of the ground, but all they did was to illuminate a sphere of mist. I later heard that as a result of this the Observer Corps reported that a plane had been shot down in flames. After no more than two or three changes of course I was in luck. The leading-out lights suddenly swung into view below. Having found them, with a heart-felt sense of relief, I was careful not to let them out of my sight, but the problem was to know the direction from which I had approached them. After a bit of circling, I decided in which direction the airfield lay. When I got back, the watch office were sending up rockets.

There was never any difficulty, as well there might have been, arising from the fact that we Army types were getting the coveted flying training on an RAF station. At all times we were treated just as if we wore blue. The instructors, however, did find us markedly different from the RAF aircrew cadets. One of them calling for his pupil over the partition in the crew-room would be answered by the stamp of feet as the soldier sprang to attention and barked out the reply of 'Sir'! This automatic reaction to orders was something the RAF had to get us out of. It did not do in the air. It was noted that we were trained to await the next order, whereas in flying one had to make one's own decisions quickly.

It was noticeable that the younger trainees, those aged around nineteen or twenty, took to flying much more readily than we old ones approaching the late twenties. It was all the more gratifying that when our log-books came back with our assessment at the end of the course, out of the four possible ratings of 'exceptional' (which practically no one received), 'above average', 'average' and 'poor', I was rated as 'above average'. It remains one of the few things I have ever been vain about.

Chapter 6

The Hotspur Glider

I last flew at Burnaston on 26 November 1942, having accumulated eighty-eight flying hours, of which thirty-five and a half were solo. On 14 December I first made the acquaintance of a glider. The next scene which presents itself to memory is that of a train chugging up a line along the Welsh Marches. There were perhaps twenty of us, some unhappy that they had not been posted to Stoke Orchard, an airfield near Cheltenham, as others of our Burnaston group had been, and were now heading away from what they thought of as civilization, into the back of beyond.

An odd recollection stays in my mind from that journey. The guard on the train was female and to my eyes not particularly young, still less attractive. As the train made its leisurely way between stations, one of my colleagues, himself not exactly an Adonis, 'took advantage of' her, shall we say, or she of him, the mailbags of the guard's compartment providing the nuptial couch. It was a mystery to me how such congress could have been agreed so speedily.

We detrained at Leominster and were conveyed to the airfield some 12 miles to the west at Shobdon, close to the foot-hills of the Welsh mountains, a countryside like the Cotswolds redolent of beautiful place-names: Eardisland, Pembridge, Staunton-on-Arrow, Golden Valley. This was No. 5 Glider Training School and there we were 'converted' on to Hotspurs.

The Hotspur glider was a beautiful little machine. If one can visualise a streamlined fuselage shaped like a slender fish, with stubby wings extending out amidships and a cocked-up tail at the back, this gives the general idea. It was made entirely of wood and glue construction. Under the wings were recessed panels or 'flaps' which could be operated by a lever in the cockpit: half-flap steepened the descent without decreasing speed, full-flap cut the forward speed and enabled the glider to be levelled out, sink on an even keel and land. The pilot and second pilot sat one behind the other right up front beneath a hinged Perspex cover. The controls were crude:

45

a spade-handled control column and foot pedals. There was only one set of these, in the front, and as a consequence flying hours recorded as second pilot had to be shown as 'passenger' in the log-book. If I remember, there were only two instruments, an altimeter and an air-speed indicator. We sat on seats shaped to take our parachutes and were of course strapped in. In its slender fuselage the Hotspur carried eight passengers, four before and four aft of the main spar. It was extremely cramped and uncomfortable in there and I do not think the glider was ever used in an operational role.[1]

I have since the war seen one, or part of one, at the Airborne Museum at Aldershot and have wondered how we ever took a machine so crudely fitted into the air. The glider had in its nose an ingenious toggle joint device which gripped the steel plug on the end of the tow rope so positively that it could not pull out, yet when the release knob in the cockpit was operated the plug detached cleanly and immediately. The tow planes were mostly Miles Masters, single-engined machines intended for the intermediate training of fighter pilots, but a few of the old-fashioned Lysanders were also being used. It was these high-wing monoplanes which, because of their short take-off and landing runs, were employed in conveying secret service agents into and out of France.[2]

Flying a glider was very different from flying a powered plane. The latter was an autonomous entity, free to climb or dive, or to turn this way or that, at your absolute will. The plane and yourself became one. You never became one with the glider. It was always in trammels, under restraint. It had to go where the tug went, like it or not, and at the tug's speed. On tow the most important thing in the world was the aeroplane in front. It had to be kept in a certain position within close limits, on the windscreen. The technique had some affinity to instrument flying.

One flew the glider directly behind the tug and slightly above. When it climbed the glider had to climb too, when it turned the glider had to follow round – an absolute case of 'whither thou goest I shall go'. In still air and straight-and-level flight it was possible to be gentle on the controls and, as it were, let the glider do the flying, but this was seldom. The air is rarely smooth, and even on a fine day there are up-currents and down-currents which one could see first give the tug a jolt as it passed through them, to be followed by a similar jolt on the glider. On normal days gusts would send the tug and glider continually up and down independently of each other, a wing would drop, the glider would slide to one side, the tow rope would slacken and then jerk tight. All this required of the glider pilot continual concentration, continual correction. On blustery days he had to fight to keep his heaving craft on an even keel and in its proper station. It could be strenuous work. The tow behind the tug was of course only part of each flight. At the end of it came the shorter crucial pull-off, free-flight and landing.

In many an account of airborne operations there is reference to the tug-plane 'releasing the glider' or 'dropping the tow'. As a generalisation this may be acceptable but in actual practice it happened only rarely and then only in an emergency. The duty of the tug was to get the glider to the LZ (Landing Zone) and put it in a position from which it could release itself with enough height over, and distance from, the objective to land safely at its appointed place. The actual release point had to be judged by the glider pilot: it was part of his skill. The tug never (except in dire emergency) 'dropped the tow': it was a point of honour, among RAF pilots at least, that they never themselves released the tow-rope whilst the glider was still attached. If the glider did not release at the expected position, this indicated that the pilot had either not identified his LZ or judged that he was not in a position to reach it. There being in the early stages no communication between the two halves of the combination, this had to be assumed from the glider's behaviour, and the tug then took it round again.

I do not think I ever heard of an authenticated case of a British pilot casting off his glider voluntarily (I emphasise British pilot), although there were stories towards the end of the war of ropes accidentally pulling out at one end or the other, which in some cases were the subject of enquiry and I believe courts-martial. Some ropes undoubtedly broke in flight. In a few cases tugs came back with the glider still on tow, when no doubt both crews had some explaining to do. I mention these points to emphasise that the decision to pull off always rested with the glider pilot alone.

After a few familiarisation exercises I went solo at the end of the month, with the second pilot's seat on this hazardous occasion being occupied by a hundredweight of sandbags, which of course presented an additional hazard if one had a head-on crash. It was the sandbag load which had killed Colonel Rock and his co-pilot when they had crashed on night-flying.

The routine of the runway was for the ground staff, which might be some of us, for we all took turns at it, to connect the rope to the glider and tug-plane, and with a winding-up motion of a flag indicate to the tug pilot that he should rev up and taxi slowly forward, taking up the slack of the rope. On the rope tightening and the glider beginning to move, the tow-master waved the flag vigorously aloft, whereupon the tug accelerated down the runway, and, allowing the glider to become airborne first, soared away into the wide blue yonder, to do whatever had been agreed with the glider pilot in advance. Because communication with the pilot of the tug with its engine running was impossible by voice, a code of signals had spontaneously developed: the flag waved horizontally near the ground meant a low release, the arm jerked upwards five times meant release at 5,000ft. So ingrained in usage did this become that when we were flying with the Yanks in Africa, it was a matter of astonishment that they could not comprehend what such obvious gesticulations meant.

The gliders were not designed to soar like sailplanes. At a gliding speed of 60–70mph they always lost height except on the odd occasion when a particularly strong up-current allowed them to retain it for a minute or two. In the hot sun of Africa the effect was more marked than in Britain and one could identify patches of ground where it was present. At Shobdon we occasionally had exceptionally clear, still evenings when it was possible to go up to perhaps 8,000ft, pull off, and with the trimmers nicely set let the glider just waft along as if on a smooth cushion of air (which is what it was) without noise and without a sense of motion.

My first night-flight was anything but propitious. According to my log-book I had had no more than three short night flights of dual instruction when, on 6 March 1943, my instructor sent me off solo. It was a dismal night, not unlike my adventure at Burnaston, but with rather more mist if anything. Shobdon had at least a tarmac runway and an electrically lit flare path, but once in the air all one had to follow was the white light in the tow plane's tail. We took off into the murk and I became disorientated. There was a light moving around on my left which I thought was another aircraft but proved to be the beacon on top of a neighbouring hill. The tug seemed to be doing unusually tight turns and once I lost him momentarily, but finally I pulled off at about the right spot on the down-wind leg parallel to the runway. This required losing height and doing two left turns, the last one into wind for the final approach.

Unfortunately, I made my last turn too soon, with the result that I was some hundreds of feet too high as I passed over the boundary fence and it looked as if I were all set to fly right out of the airfield and into the blackness on the other side. I was losing height as quickly as I could, but, thinking I would never land on the runway, for some reason decided I ought put the glider down in an area to one side and beyond it. The ground was of course invisible.

Continuing to lose height and flying far too fast, I suddenly felt an enormous bump. I thought I was down, but there was none of the usual part-heard, part-felt rumbling of the wheels. I was in a sort of vacuum, with no noise, no air-speed and nothing to be felt on the control column. In fact I had bounced high in the air. Bang I came down, up again and down again, totally out of control, and apparently did a series of kangaroo-like jumps which took me in a ground-loop right onto the runway which I had done my best to avoid. I sat there shaken, hardly believing I was still in one piece. An officer, one of ours, drove up in a jeep. Far from enquiring as to my health and well-being, or even commenting on my unorthodox landing, he curtly told me off for obstructing the runway.

I flew by night again a week later and all went well thereafter. As regulations required, I reported the heavy landing and submitted a damage report, but no particular notice was taken of the incident. In spite of its antics, the glider survived except for some broken wood near the tail. This says something about how strongly they were made. I have a piece of Hotspur HH257 still.

Considering the intrinsically dangerous nature of what we were doing it is surprising that accidents were rare. Some people misjudged their approach and landed short (I did once but just managed to get into a distant corner of the airfield), whilst others 'landed away', as we satirically called their involuntary descent, but in most cases without damage. In one case, when a tow rope broke, the pilots landed on a steep hillside, the glider broke up, and they just opened the cockpit cover and stepped out on to the grass beside them. This sort of experience gave us great confidence in the ability of these wooden machines to withstand impact. None of my group was ever hurt. One of them, however, killed an unfortunate aircraftsman who was incautiously walking on the runway whilst the glider swept in noiselessly behind him in the dark.

The Regiment contained a number of ex-RAF pilots. Colonel Chatterton was one of these, and he had been grounded for medical reasons which no longer applied. It was rumoured that some of the others had flown for the fascists in the Spanish Civil War which had disqualified them from further service in the RAF. Alastair had been commissioned in the Fleet Air Arm, but why he was now a corporal in the Glider Pilot Regiment

I never found out, a man's past being a closed book, as in the French Foreign Legion. The last I heard of him was after the war when he was managing a mine in South America.

All activity, however exciting, can become a bit of a routine after a while, and so it was with flying. At one stage one of the instructors, who was known as a bit of a daredevil, tried to loop and then slow-roll a Hotspur. This was really forbidden because the plane was not stressed to fly upside down. Another man and I tried to do the same but did not get the glider over and just stalled out of it. Tow pilots found the work especially boring, and used to divert themselves, and us, by exceptionally low flying. A favourite prank was to approach the Malvern Hills at a reasonable height over normal ground level, so that we just whistled over the summit with few feet clear, causing any unfortunate civilian walking there to dive for safety. I once had a trip as passenger in a Lysander on which the pilot positively brushed the treetops with his wheels, with a glider hanging on behind. On another occasion in a Miles Magister the pilot let me fly from the back seat whilst he had a rest.[3]

This familiarity sometimes bred disaster. A friend of mine from Burnaston days was 'stooging around', as we called alleged navigation exercises, over Salisbury Plain in a later stage of our training, when the plane just dived into the ground, killing both him and his co-pilot. It was thought that each had thought the other was doing the flying, so that when the plane dived each believed the other was playing a prank, until it was too late to pull out.

The village nearest Shobdon was Pembridge. We heard that the vicar and his lady kept open house for servicemen during most evenings, and Alastair and I went down there once or twice. Because of the distance we had to cycle. It was the depths of winter and very dark, and there was a great shortage of batteries for cycle lamps. One evening we cycled round for a cup of tea and a read of the newspapers, and then back round the aerodrome to our hut. On the way back we fell into a trap set by two policemen, were summonsed, and each fined 30 shillings for not having rear lights. The case was brought at Kington, some distance away, and we wrote to answer the charge. Afterwards I regretted that we had not contested it in person, as it was quite preposterous, considering the risks we were taking by day and night and the impossibility of obtaining batteries, that such a petty charge should be laid. And 30 shillings was a lot of money in those days.

At the conclusion of this course I received a flying rating of Average and 72 marks. I had added on 72¾ hours to my flying time. After this further step in our progress we were taken to Bulford, the big old Army camp on Salisbury Plain, for a few days. Colonel Chatterton suddenly appeared for the presentation of our wings. This was not a very prestigious affair. We were paraded between two huts, the Colonel addressed us briefly and handed each the coveted insignia, and, it being a freezing cold morning, one of our gallant number fell in a dead faint. This was regarded as not at all the right thing for a Total Soldier. We also received promotion to sergeant. Whilst this was to recognise our status as qualified pilots, an additional purpose was to increase our rate of pay. At one stage we were said to be, rank for rank, the highest paid people in the Army. Three days after leaving Shobdon we were flying Horsas at Brize Norton, Oxfordshire.

Chapter 7

The Horsa Glider

The Horsa was the operational glider at that time. It had begun to be produced in quantity about a year before we met, and it was the vehicle in which we would, in due course, go to war.

At first sight it was an ungainly beast, quite unlike the lissom Hotspur. As it sat on the runway, with its nose wheel probing the ground, it looked like a huge crouching insect, and all the more so because most planes those days had their third wheel at the rear and sloped backwards. The design was very simple. For most of its length the body was a large cylinder, high enough to stand up in, with a greenhouse-like cockpit covering most of the front and tapering aft to a lofty tail-fin and rudder. Inside, across the cabin roof, ran the great main spar. The wings were thick and provided with flaps the size of barn doors. These could be lowered, like those of the Hotspur, into two positions: about 40 degrees and almost vertical.

In the cockpit the controls were few and crude. The two 'sticks', one for each pilot, moved fore and aft and had wheel-like handles for lateral control. There were foot pedals for the rudder and wheel-brakes, a wheel for the trimmers, and levers for the flaps and the tow-release gear. An altimeter and an air-speed indicator, together with a gauge showing pressure in the compressed air bottle which powered the brakes and flaps, comprised the instrument panel. Later a gadget like an artificial horizon was added. This was a most crude device, operated merely by an elastic cord that led to the yoke of the tow rope and was supposed to give, by means of vertical and horizontal crossed lines, an indication of the glider's position behind the tug-plane, the all-important factor. We called it the 'angle of dangle', and because of its inaccuracy never liked it very much.[1]

The Horsa stood quite high off the ground supported by an under-carriage of heavy steel spars with two small rubber-tyred wheels. The early models had a broad skid between the wheels, designed with the intention that, the whole undercart having been jettisoned, the glider could slither to a halt. Unfortunately the locking mechanism proved faulty, so that in some cases the undercarriage released itself, and, bouncing back from the ground, took away portions of the tail-plane, with disastrous results. In one incident, part of the undercarriage embedded itself in one of the wings and the pilots flew all the way from Cornwall to Africa like that, the glider all but not quite un-flyable. Later the skid idea was dropped and the undercarriage permanently secured.

Unusually for that time for such a large load-carrying aircraft, the body and wings of the Horsa were entirely made of wood. The skin, ribs, stringers and spars were of laminated timber of varying thicknesses, glued together. One could see where the milky adhesive had oozed out of the joints. The whole was immensely strong. In the new models there was the pleasing smell of resinous timber.

I will try to give an impression of what it was like to fly this unconventional aircraft. It was a heavy machine, weighing I believe about three tons unladen but double that with its load of thirty armed men, or equipment of similar weight. The pilots sat side by side in the cockpit, the Perspex windscreen giving more than 180 degrees visibility all round and nearly as much vertically. Compared with the narrow cockpits of the Tiger Moth and the Hotspur, it caused one to feel very much exposed. The first pilot sat on the right. There was a door behind and between the pilots which communicated with the cabin where the load was, in which the officer or NCO in charge of the latter often used to station himself so that he could see what was going on and talk to the pilots.

The load, if it were 'live', sat on benches along each side with their trailers and other equipment in the centre. They and it were strapped or lashed down, a necessary precaution in a conveyance which was pitching and rolling about all the time. During long flights the soldiers often used to while the time away by playing cards. Some of them were sick, which led to a weeding out in respect of airborne activities. Their only 'convenience', a very elementary one, was a rubber pipe with a funnel at its upper end into which they could relieve themselves. What happened if they got 'taken short' otherwise I never knew.

In training we had parachutes in the initial stages, but with 'live load' aboard and on operations we and they were without them. I think the idea was that if the load could not have parachutes, the pilots should not have them either, in case they made their escape leaving the load to their fate. We never worried about this, but I remember one instructor who insisted on leaving the exit door open whilst he flew so that he could escape at a moment's notice. For our part we had, as I have mentioned with Hotspurs, great confidence in our aircraft, and preferred the idea of crashing with them to the obnoxious one of parachuting out. Paratroops held entirely the opposite view. The technique was said to be to put a wing in first and let that absorb the shock if a crash became inevitable.

Having taken off successfully and achieved its prescribed altitude, the glider had the choice of going into high or low tow. The dividing line was the tug's slipstream. To get down to low tow, one informed the tug (if there was any means of communicating with him, which in most cases there was not), and gently put the control column forward, and the glider then entered a stream of very turbulent air churned up by the tug's engines. If there were four of these, as with the great Halifaxes which were used later, the turbulence was very rough indeed. In the slipstream the glider swung and twisted about, and, the controls being not exactly precision-built and taking a measurable period of time to respond, one had to anticipate as far as possible how far the wing would drop or the glider slew round before applying the opposite movement. But the Horsa, by reason of its high wing design, had excellent 'pendulum stability', i.e. it returned to level flight as soon as it was able to do so. Some, however, had a built-in bias with one wing or the other wanting to drop all the time. The 'erks' (or aircraftsmen) used to compensate for this simply by stuffing sandbags into the opposite wing!

A lot, indeed nearly everything, depended on fore and aft stability, which could be greatly impaired by uneven loading. The frames or ribs were numbered and in the office was a brass cut-out model which was designed to enable the weight to be put on each one to be calculated. Naturally this was of no use – we did not know the weight of jeeps, ramps, ammunition trailers and all the other pieces of impedimenta – and the problem had to be solved by judgement alone. Firstly, the disposition of the various parts of the load had to look right; secondly the pilot and his mate would go round to the tail, hang on to the struts and try to bounce the nose-wheel off the ground. If this succeeded the load was positioned correctly. Crude though it was, the test was accurate enough.

A glider which was nose or tail-heavy was difficult or impossible to fly. During the German airborne invasion of Crete a whole Command HQ was lost as a result of incautious loading. The Horsas were designed to have a relatively short flying life, about thirty hours I believe, but in due course many greatly exceeded this figure. Later on there were incidents in which part of the tail assembly gave way in the air, killing all aboard. We were then instructed, as part of the pre-flight check, to put our shoulders under the enormous rudder and try to heave it upwards. If it gave more than three inches the aircraft was unserviceable. However, declaring an aircraft unserviceable was regarded as bad form. I tried to do it only once and got into a blazing row with the ground crew about it.

A misconception about flying gliders was that it was quiet in the air owing to the absence of engine noise. This was quite untrue. On tow they were very noisy. Being dragged through the air at speeds of up to 160mph, the vibration and rushing of air along the fuselage reminded me of the sounds of a train in the London Underground. There were creaks and groans from the overstressed fabric and one's ears were always cocked for some failure, a habit which is with me still and takes away a lot of the pleasure of flying. It was hard work too: keeping the heavy machine straight and level and in position behind the tug took a good deal of strength.

When we became experienced, however, the noise and sensation of the air coursing along the fuselage could be put to advantage. This sounds like an old pilot's tale, but it was possible to fly, in low tow, to some extent by the feel of the tug's slipstream on the glider's roof. One could, if the air was otherwise relatively still, position the glider where one just sensed the slipstream rumbling above; a little lower and one lost it altogether, a little higher and one was buffeted about. This trick was very useful when flying at night with only the tug's lights for guidance.

After considerable practice and application to the task, we developed the skill to put even a heavily loaded glider gently and precisely down where it was meant to be, which was the whole object of the training. I remember a dozen of us flying at Leicester East. It was a Friday after-noon and the RAF Warrant Officer responsible for securing the gliders for the weekend asked us not to leave them all over the airfield from which his 'erks' would have to retrieve them with a tractor, a time-taking task. Returning from a cross-country flight we put the gliders down in a neat bunch just outside the hangar doors, much to the RAF's amazement. The fact that the Horsa could be towed fast and landed slowly represented great expertise on the designers' part. Its steep controlled descent was I think unequalled by any other aircraft.

Our Heavy Glider Course at Brize Norton lasted until 6 April 1943 and according to my log-book was very intensive. I recall two episodes which are worth recounting. On one occasion I had a flight in a Whitley and occupied the rear gunner's position. The guns had been removed but the rest of the mechanism was in place and one could traverse the turret and go through the motions of engaging the enemy. It gave me some idea of the absolute loneliness the gunner must have felt during operations, especially at night. He was out beyond the tail-plane, separated from the rest of the crew and totally exposed.

The other episode involved an officer. Although the gap between the commissioned and non-commissioned was narrowing in our outfit as we all had the same role in the air, it was rigidly maintained on the ground, and this officer came from one of the more prestigious regiments, the Hussars I think. On one or two occasions he sent for me to accompany him on flights as co-pilot, regarding me as a steady type I suppose. I had no particular objection to this except that if one were to judge from the fumes with which he filled the cockpit, he had usually calmed his nerves with whisky in advance.

On one flight we started out with a reasonably clear sky but on the way back the clouds began to gather and we found ourselves above an ever-thickening bank. Now at that time flying a glider in cloud was considered an impossibility and certainly was a dangerous thing to do, and the best my tug pilot could do was to make for a hole below and carry out a slow descending turn. So we followed him down as if into a vortex and inevitably soon found ourselves in the cloud absolutely blind. We could not even see the tow rope.

The officer, I regret to say, panicked. 'Pull off, pull off,' he yelled, and made for the release lever. I did not much like the idea of making a forced landing, and in any case we had plenty of height, so I told him in actual terms not to be a bloody fool. After some long minutes the murk lightened and we suddenly came out below the cloud into daylight. We were still on tow, but where was the tug? Wildly looking around, I discerned it nowhere near where it ought to have been, but down below and behind us, with the rope curling back in a great S-bend.

The problem was now to get down into the normal place behind the tug. Some vague recollection came into my mind that one could slow an aircraft down by 'fish-tailing' it, i.e. swinging it so that first one broadside and then the other was presented to the direction of flight. This is what I did with the cumbersome machine and everything came right. I don't remember the officer saying very much about our adventure, but he never bore me any ill-will for what would have been gross insubordination on the ground. The incident was unusual enough to be reported on and I discussed it with the tug pilot who was a good deal apologetic (though it was hardly his fault). I later wondered whether it was one of the reasons why I was again assessed as 'above average' at the end of this course.

There followed a gap now of six weeks until the middle of May when I did no flying. It was one of the unsatisfactory aspects of our training that from now on it became spasmodic, allowing one to lose 'form', which one did very easily, and get out of practice.

Since our departure from Tilshead, the Regiment had been assigned a base in a desolate part of Salisbury Plain, near the artillery ranges at Larkhill. This, Fargo Camp, provided no more than the most rudimentary facilities: Chatterton more or less apologised for putting us there and asked us to do our best with it. It was a far cry from well-appointed Brize Norton and devoid of any connection with the air. Life became again a matter of parades and inspections, physical training both in the gym and outside, and marches.

After some while flying was again organised. We were taken daily by coach to Netheravon, not far away, to fly Hotspurs and Tiger Moths. Netheravon was a very old-established aerodrome, one of the first I believe. The field was of grass and had the characteristic of several dips and humps which were not too inconvenient for small powered planes but for gliders meant that the tug aircraft more or less disappeared from sight during the take-off. We experienced here a sort of apartheid, and the only facility of the station we were allowed to use, and that only informally, was a beehive-shaped little building where one could get simulated gunnery practice with films of attacking aircraft projected on the wall.

Netheravon had been used for experimental flying. We saw a prototype Hengist glider there which was midway between a Hotspur and a Horsa but never went into production, and experiments were made with snatching gliders from the ground to solve the problem of retrieval. It never became practicable with Horsas, though the Americans achieved it with the smaller and lighter Wacos (or Hadrians as they were called over here) and it was used for unloaded Horsas on a small scale.[2]

The war was now taking an upward turn. The Germans were exhausting their strength in Russia. The Americans had decided – and this is one of the most significant decisions ever to be made concerning our country's history – to throw their main military effort into finishing the war in

Europe before dealing with Japan. The first major British and Commonwealth victory had been achieved with the defeat of the Germans at El Alamein in October and November 1942, and this was followed, in the latter month, by the Anglo-US landing on the western coast of North Africa. By May 1943 North Africa had been cleared of the enemy. The next step was to cross the narrow waters of the Mediterranean and take the battle into Italy.

Thus, in the spring of 1943 there was at last the feeling of optimism in the country. The hitherto undefeated Germans had proved defeatable. Arms, equipment, supplies of all kinds were now available, apparently in unlimited quantities; new planes were in the air; United States soldiers of both sexes were seen on the streets, not always with approval. After a long period of baffled frustration – and only those who lived through it can appreciate what it was like to be in an impoverished island which a merciless enemy was almost succeeding in cutting off from the rest of the world – the future was beginning to open up again. Victory, release from physical danger for oneself and one's family, the lifting of restrictions, the prospect of one day resuming one's career and normal life, all now began to look if not certain, at least probable. Military initiative was now possible on our side.

Chapter 8

Overseas

Following the completion of our glider training and an interlude at Netheravon, we were suddenly issued with tropical kit and sent off to the Mediterranean. Part of the Regiment was already out there, and just as we arrived was having its first experience of real live warfare in the invasion of Sicily which took place on 9 July 1943. This was an Anglo-US enterprise and for various reasons proved a highly expensive one. Through no fault of theirs, many of the gliders were unable to reach the coast and out of the 130 which set out only twelve landed on their intended targets. These and the others which managed to get down on dry land created enough havoc to assist what was undoubtedly a great success overall, but eighty-eight glider pilots were casualties. By any standard this is a very high rate of casualties.[1] However, we only came in on the tail-end of this, and my visit to this theatre of war proved in the event to be little more than a trip around the Mediterranean at the government's expense. I shall consequently not linger over this part of my memoirs, confining myself to a few impressions or flashbacks which the reader is welcome to skip if they wish.

We embarked at Liverpool on the *Dunera*, a ship which had gained an unfortunate notoriety as the one used to remove the so-called 'enemy aliens', i.e. mainly German-Jewish refugees in Britain, who had more personal reasons to hate the Nazis than we had, to Canada under Churchill's infamous 'collar the lot' directive. The ship was incredibly crowded; even to get to a wash-basin for a shave was an achievement. We slept in hammocks, which, once one had found the knack of getting in and then staying in, were remarkably comfortable. The sight of hundreds of them swinging in unison as the ship rolled was quite extraordinary. Some evenings we played cards or Monopoly with the crew who regaled us with stories of the effects of underwater explosions on the human body: apparently, they could break every bone in the body without killing the victim. To add point to these yarns we heard depth-charges going off most nights, reminding us that the North Atlantic was a dangerous place.

The voyage took about three weeks. We had apparently sailed almost over to the American coast to avoid the U-boats, but we did not see anything of it. Our first sight of Africa was Algiers harbour, where we arrived early one morning. I remember looking at this then-legendary town (this was well before the era of mass-tourism) and thinking of its violent history and how it was on the edge of the mysterious 'Dark Continent' which stretched through desert and jungle and savannah right down to the Cape of Good Hope. There was still a place for wonder in those days. The hope that we might see something of Algiers was disappointed when we were disembarked, only to be marched round the harbour to be stowed away in the bowels of another ship. This was the *Christobal*, one of the assembly-line Liberty Ships which had the reputation of breaking in half in a storm. The guns had rust in the barrels, clearly demonstrating that she was not a Royal Navy vessel, but we never saw a gun-crew anyway.

Sometimes we would hitch a lift into Philippeville, the only amenity of which was a canteen staffed by French girls, some of exceptional beauty. They had eyes, however, only for the Americans, who looked, spoke and deported themselves like film-stars.

One morning I was at breakfast in the mess-tent when my head began to swim. The canvas walls began to stir with a peculiar heavy and languorous motion, and a blast of heat as from a suddenly-opened furnace door filled the place. Wildly, for a moment I thought that the cookhouse was on fire, but this was the wind off the desert, the sirocco. For a day or two I was prostrate and could do nothing but rest uncomfortably in my tent. It soon passed off, all part of the process of acclimatisation I suppose.

Next we were taken in lorry-loads over the mountains into Tunisia. Bleaker, emptier country I have never known, yet when we stopped Arabs materialised as if from nowhere. They sold to our men scraggy chickens which they brought out live and nicked in the jugular vein with a knife before throwing them on the ground to bleed to death. One poor bird in its agony fluttered four feet into the air dropping blood. We passed shot-down planes stripped of everything useful, and occasionally little groups of graves marking the place where guns had been in action. In one place there were Arabs living in holes in the ground.

Our next camp was at a place called Msaken a mile or two outside Sousse on the Tunisian coast. Here our billet was the olive groves where we settled down, two men to a tree. At night the hanging mosquito nets looked like gravestones. There was a tent or two for meals and squadron office, but not much else. It was here that the pilots who had taken part in the Sicily operation rejoined us. They had seemingly been scattered all over the Mediterranean. Most had grim stories, when they were prepared to tell them, of towlines being dropped by the tugs when they were too far from shore to have a hope of reaching it. Those that did get down inevitably hit rocks or the stone walls with which Sicily abounds. One day General Hopkinson called us all, Montgomery-wise, into a circle and asked us not to go beating up the Yanks who had provided most of the planes used for parachute dropping and glider-towing in this operation. The Anglo-US alliance was too important, he said, for that.

A constant source of temptation was the remains of a blown-up ammunition dump not far away. Shells, grenades, small-arms ammunition lay around in vast quantities, all probably in an unstable condition. Someone had a Luger pistol which we had endless ammunition to play around with. One man received severe burns to his body from incautiously handling a phosphorous grenade. The place was strictly out-of-bounds of course.

Towards the end of July we started flying again. We were taken daily to an airstrip nearby where we were introduced by British instructors to American Waco (or Hadrian) gliders. These machines were quite unlike the Horsas, not only in construction and load capacity but also in handling characteristics. They were made of metal tubes covered by canvas – not a good structure for crashing in – and had a long flat approach glide, controlled by spoilers rather than flaps, which made spot-on landings an impossibility. The airstrip being of dirt, so much of it was blown into the air by the slipstream of the tug that it was impossible to see it on take-off. One just headed into the dust-cloud aiming at where one supposed the tug to be and as soon as possible rose above it.

Soon after, great activity began. An operation was imminent. Weapons, ammunition and kit were issued, and our 'load' of soldiers from the Ox and Bucks Light Infantry came into camp near the airfield. Then just as suddenly, it all evaporated. I have since found out what was at the back of this. As part of the plan for the invasion of Italy, which eventually was a sea-borne operation at Salerno on 9 September, we were being prepared for an assault on Rome. It was decided at the last moment that there were too many German forces defending the area. Had the assault gone ahead, a probable if minor result would have been that my bones would now be resting in a graveyard somewhere near the Eternal City.

However, we were to take part in an invasion of sorts. Having been taken up to Bizerta, where we swam in the harbour among sunken ships, we embarked on a comfortable Dutch passenger vessel (the *Princess Beatrix*, I think) and after a delightful voyage, which included sleeping on deck in the moonlight, arrived at the port of Taranto in the heel of Italy. We were in fact part of the occupation/invasion force which had started to arrive on 9 September, three days in advance of us. All was quiet when we disembarked. Evidence of war was not lacking, as corpses were bobbing about in the harbour from the wreck of HMS *Abdiel*, a mine-layer, which had picked up a magnetic mine and been blown up with the loss of forty-eight naval personnel and 120 officers and men from the 2nd Paras whom she had been carrying. There was also a collapsed building in the middle of the town, an apartment block with an air-raid shelter beneath, from which the smell increased daily.

Soon we were moved a short way up-country, allegedly to help form a defensive line around the city. The enemy at that time were nowhere to be seen, having removed themselves 40 miles away. Life here now became idyllic. We lived in unspoilt olive groves under the shade of the trees, drawing water from an antique well (until later troops stupidly fouled it) and swimming in a crystal brook (spoilt eventually by the drowning of an Indian soldier – how sad and curious that he had come all that way to meet his Nemesis there). In nearby vineyards the grape harvest was ripe and we were allowed the freedom of them. Never before or since have I seen such grapes, full, round and sugar-sweet, hanging in enormous bunches. Whether our bodies were craving some vitamin the grapes provided I do not know, but the grapes became an obsession. Having gorged all afternoon we still took scarves-full back to our camp for the night.

One day a friend of mine asked me if I would like to see the inside of a brothel; how he had found out about it, or rather them, for he knew of two, I never realised, but I am quite certain that he had not patronised them. The first was quite astonishing, as it was a municipal one. (One has to remind oneself that they do things differently in other countries.) The entrance was a tiled corridor, just like that of a public lavatory, and in the entrance hall sat a lady at a reception desk from whom one bought, for a very small fee, an entrance ticket in the form of a small plastic disc like a tiddlywink. Further along was another tiled corridor with cubicles partitioned off. The whole place was seething with soldiers, most of them extremely young, with here and there an Italian among them, but they were behaving in an outrageous fashion, banging on the doors to tell their mates to hurry up and climbing the partitions to see what was going on, on the other side. Such glimpses of the cubicles as one could obtain revealed that they had iron beds covered in rough brown blankets, with oilcloth placed over the end as a protection against the clients' boots, apparently no interval being allowed to take them off. My sympathy went out to the harassed hard-working women, obviously doing their level best to keep up with the demand. It was a pitiable sight. The other establishment, a private one, made some concession to elegance. The set-up was the same, with Madame sitting at the receipt of custom in the hall. There were only two girls there, one a dismal-looking woman swathed in a dressing gown, the other, much younger, garbed as a chorus girl. As to temptation, it was absolutely nil.

Specialised troops like ourselves were apparently not approved of by some of the higher-ups. (Chatterton tells of an incident in this connection in his book.) The message filtered down to us that the commanding officer of the 1st Airborne Division, under whose control we now were, thought there was nothing much to flying gliders and that it was on a par with driving a car. The paratroops had been used in a purely infantry role in Africa and the same thing was going to happen to us. As a result we suddenly found ourselves dispatched on toughening-up marches across rough country. I remember some officer standing in a jeep yelling at us to 'double', something we were quite incapable of doing at that stage. However, this phase ended as suddenly as it had begun. I imagine Chatterton was not going to have his men turned into ordinary foot-sloggers.

Another move and we found ourselves at a small town called Putignano, housed in the splendid Edificio Scolastico. Here I had a visitor. This was Captain Bernard Clarke, my brother-in-law. How he traced me I do not know. It was a little embarrassing as I had no possible means of entertaining him as his rank required, and all I could do was take him into our billet, where we lived entirely at floor level, and introduce him to my comrades. All went well, however. I was able to tell him about his son whom I had seen grow into a little boy, whilst his own memory of him was as an infant in arms nearly four years earlier. It was to be another three years before Bernard saw either my sister or their son again.

Putignano had formerly been a fortified city on the top of a hill and although the walls had been replaced by a wide ring road, the interior was a maze of medieval streets. One day one of my comrades asked me to go along with him as he had been offered a Biretta automatic pistol for sale and was going to collect it. Threading our way through the narrow lanes we came to the address given. It turned out to be the police station, the vendor being the local Chief of Police.

Autumn was now coming on and there was a distinct chill in the air in the evenings. The food was worse than we ever had had or would ever have again. There was tinned American bacon, mostly fat, corned beef ditto, tinned potatoes, with the appearance, texture and taste of wax, oleo-margarine, white tasteless bread and jam from Tel Aviv which had never seen fruit. Of real fruit and vegetables there were none.

After a brief call at Syracuse, with a view of Mount Etna, we sailed again half way across the Atlantic, enjoying fine weather until the green hills of Northern Ireland hove in sight; then it rained. We had got back in a cold December and were shipped straight over to Skegness in Lincolnshire. Someone had told me that to drink any alcohol within six months would be fatal, but the warm English pubs and the English beer were, after so long an absence, not to be refused. I suffered no after-effects, became fully fit, and on 16 December 1943 was flying again.

Chapter 9

D-Day, 6 June 1944

During the spring of 1944 the Allies were engaged in extremely bitter fighting as they slowly pushed up through Italy. Meanwhile a vast build-up of US forces and supplies was taking place in England in preparation for an invasion of occupied North-West Europe. Ever since the summer of 1942, the Germans had been expecting an invasion, but they were not sure when and where it would happen and elaborate deception plans hatched by the Allies further served to disrupt the enemy's defensive strategy.

Under the direction of General Eisenhower, the Supreme Allied Commander, Operation Overlord would be finally launched on 6 June 1944. In the largest amphibious operation in history, 1,200 ships and some 4,000 assault craft would deliver over 125,000 men onto the Normandy beaches during the first twenty-four hours of the operation.

On the western flank of the invasion US paratroopers from the 82nd and 101st Airborne Divisions would land north of Carentan, at the base of the Cotentin Peninsula, while two US infantry and ranger divisions would advance over the beaches known as Utah and Omaha. Meanwhile, to the east, two British divisions would land at Sword and Gold Beaches and a Canadian division would land at Juno.

As US forces assaulted the western sector, the 6th British Airborne Division was tasked with landing on the edge of the eastern flank and securing the boundary from enemy counter-attacks. This vital role, which helped to secure the allied bridgehead, involved dropping and landing airborne forces close to the Caen Canal and the parallel River Orne, both of which entered the English Channel adjacent to the town of Ouistreham. About 4 miles upriver two bridges had to be captured in order to control these waterways and secure the road towards Ouistreham. So the initial objective of the 6th Airborne Division was to capture the Bénouville Bridge (subsequently called Pegasus Bridge), which spanned the Caen Canal, and Ranville Bridge (known as Horsa Bridge) to the east, which crossed the

67

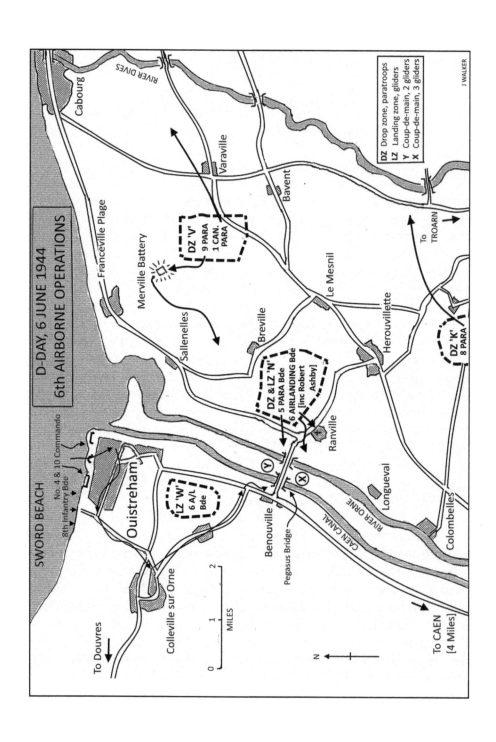

SWORD BEACH

D-DAY, 6 JUNE 1944
6th AIRBORNE OPERATIONS

RIVER DIVES

Cabourg

Franceville Plage

Varaville

Bavent

Merville Battery

DZ 'V'
9 PARA
1 CAN.
PARA

Sallenelles

Le Mesnil

Breville

Herouvillette

To TROARN

DZ 'K'
8 PARA

DZ & LZ 'N'
5 PARA Bde
6 AIRLANDING Bde
[inc Robert
Ashby]

Ranville

Longueval

Colombelles

No. 4 & 10 Commando

8th Infantry Bde

Ouistreham

LZ 'W'
6 A/L
Bde

Benouville

Pegasus Bridge

CAEN CANAL

RIVER ORNE

Colleville sur Orne

To Douvres

0   1   2
MILES

N

To CAEN
[4 Miles]

DZ Drop zone, paratroops
LZ Landing zone, gliders
Y   Coup-de-main, 2 gliders
X   Coup-de-main, 3 gliders

J WALKER

River Orne. The airborne troops were to hold these bridges until relieved by units of No. 1 Special Service (Commando) Brigade, commanded by Brigadier Lord Lovat.[1]

After reinforcements had landed in adjacent dropping/landing zones, the Paras were to carry out the second objective of assaulting the massive gun battery at Merville, near the mouth of the river. The third objective was to destroy a number of bridges that lay to the east, over the River Dives. This was to be carried out with the aid of the Royal Engineers, thereby cutting off expected attacks from the 12th SS and 21st Panzer Divisions, known to be in the region.

Regarding the first objective, Major John Howard and his detachment from the 2nd Battalion, Oxfordshire and Buckinghamshire Light Infantry, were to land in three Horsas at 0020 hrs and deliver a lightning strike on Pegasus Bridge. Three other gliders would simultaneously deliver more Ox and Bucks' sections to capture the nearby Horsa Bridge. Once these two bridges were taken, 5 Para Brigade would be dropped into Zone 'N', just to the north of the nearby village of Ranville. At the same time, 3 Para Brigade would descend on Zone 'V' towards the coastal battery of Merville. Several hours later sixty-eight Horsas and four Hamilcars were to land on this same Zone 'N' bringing in the HQ 6th Airborne, together with units of the Royal Engineers and Royal Artillery and their equipment and light guns. In all, ninety-eight gliders would take part. By then, the zones would be littered with crashed gliders, parachutes and general battlefield detritus which could pose a problem for incoming gliders. There were also plenty of anti-glider poles remaining, which needed to be flattened, so included in the second lift of sixty-eight Horsas and four Hamilcars, planned to come in at 0320 hrs, was a Horsa piloted by Robert Ashby. It contained a small bull-dozer and its team, which on landing would be employed in clearing away the obstacles and debris to allow more gliders to land.[2]

In the early hours of 6 June the US airborne units encountered heavy enemy flak on their journey to the western sector of the invasion zone and the large air armada was split up. Many US paratroopers were dropped far beyond their target zones, while others perished inside enemy lines or fell into rivers and drowned. They fought bravely and eventually managed to re-group and there are grounds for believing that their scattered deployment further confused the Germans as to the true direction of the invasion.[3] *Meanwhile, US infantry and ranger units encountered stiff resistance at*

Omaha and suffered very heavy casualties on the beach before eventually capturing the bluffs. The Americans achieved more rapid progress on Utah beach, where their infantry units soon managed to secure the beachhead and begin their link-up with airborne forces inland.

Meanwhile on the eastern flank, the 6th British Airborne enjoyed remarkable initial success. Just after midnight on 5/6 June, after some skilful piloting, six gliders landed close to the two target bridges and after skirmishing with the enemy, Major Howard and his men secured them after ten minutes. German resistance soon stiffened and as further airborne troops landed they became engaged in fierce fighting in and around the nearby hamlets and villages. Army and Royal Marine commandos, who later fought their way up from the beaches, joined them in clearing houses, bunkers and strongpoints. It was the prelude to weeks of heavy fighting as the Allies pushed out from their beachhead.

*   *   *

D-Day started for us when, one morning early in February 1944, we were put into a wooden hut at Thruxton aerodrome with a lot of new people and told to choose our second pilots. Second pilots were men who had volunteered for and been accepted by the GPR but for whom full training facilities were not then available. In their months of waiting, disappointed as they were, they had had their time filled with so-called 'air experience', which meant acting as 'live load' to those of us who were ahead.

My second pilot, Jim Donaldson, chose me rather than I him. Apparently, he had flown with me in my Shobdon days, and though I could not recall him, he had remembered me as someone he might get along with. The first pilot/second pilot concept merits a comment. It was derived partly from the 'crewing-up' practice of the RAF for bomber aircrews, but more I think from the 'buddy-buddy' system of the American Army with which Chatterton had become involved in North Africa.[4]

Chattie wanted to create the idea of a team. Thus, Chattie to Air Vice Marshal Hollinghurst, Commander, 38 Group, RAF:

> You know that your best aircrews are a team: pilots, navigators, forward and rear-gunners and engineers, understanding each other perfectly. Well, sir, now you have two extra – the glider pilots – on the end of the rope ... Within reason the glider pilots must live on the airfields, with your own aircrews – live, drink, laugh and

womanize with them. It is only in this way that they will really come to understand each other, and the air, as well.[5]

It did not work out quite like that. We and they had different roles, and in any case our trips were one-way, but some vestige of the idea caught on, and once we were assigned to a tug (which was immediately before an operation) there seemed to grow up a sort of proprietary fellow feeling between us and them, but it went no further.

Between us glider pilots the relationship was all that Chattie had hoped for. We did most things together: trained together, ate together, slept in adjoining beds, and went out on the town together. Donaldson was a Scot from Dundee and, like many Scots, he had more intelligence and education than would have been found in someone in his station in life, which was that of a jobbing plasterer, in the south. He was somewhat older than the rest, and we made a good team. I gave him as much flying training as I could and more than most second pilots got, for which he was always grateful. After the war, having emigrated to Kenya where he became a water bailiff, he died suddenly in his early forties.

I remember a strange episode on a warm spring day, when, some of the cruder spirits finding a swan incubating an egg, they drove the poor thing off its nest and stole the egg. Scrambled, it tasted egg-like and very filling. I can still remember the look of crestfallen dignity on that poor swan's face after this robbery.

Another incident did not have a happy ending. We were flying at Hampstead Norris, an informal grass airfield deep in the country near Newbury. On the night in question, a still moonlit one, the usual routine was taking place, beginning with a 'weather test', for which one of the Whitleys flew a circuit or two to see what the visibility was like.[6] I went up as a passenger – one tended to take every opportunity for 'air experience' and for 'getting one's eye in'. We completed our night circuits in the gliders and Jim and I were walking back to our billet when the engine note of a Whitley still flying made us stop and listen. Our ears had by now become very sensitive to variations of aircraft noise. The plane got further and further away instead of doing its usual circuits, then there was a moment's silence followed by a hollow bump. The plane had crashed.

It transpired that due to faulty maintenance something had progressively created a blockage in the pitot head, the tube facing forward which operated the airspeed indicator. As this gave lower and lower readings (and in a heavy powered plane to have enough airspeed is critical), the pilot had put his nose further and further down until he had piled into a hillside. All aboard were killed except the man in the rear-gunner's turret, who had a broken back. The glider had pulled off at the last moment and had made a safe emergency landing. I was later told that this was the plane in which I had gone up earlier for the weather test. Although there was an enquiry and the cause of the crash established, I never heard that blame was attached to anyone. Such things happened in the war.

There were many bright clear evenings at Hampstead Norris that spring, and they were usually filled with processions of bombers going out on night raids over Germany. For hours it seemed, and as far as the eye could reach, plane followed plane across the sky as the day waned. I used to send up an unspoken prayer for the young men up there, well knowing that some would never come back.

After a time our training began to concentrate upon putting down a group of gliders, sometimes light, sometimes heavy, in an area marked out on the runway. We were no longer a training unit, but 'B Squadron', which consisted of three 'flights' each of some forty-four officers and NCOs. Unfortunately, the cryptic names of the various exercises do not reveal what they actually consisted of, but we certainly refined the technique of landing close together and bunching up on the ground, sometimes doing this at night without lights. The later ones are named 'strips' in my log-book. Significantly we once did an exercise called 'Dawn Flying'.

At length the purpose of the 'strip' and other exercises was revealed. We were taken to a very secret place well away from the public eye and there shown lines of thick sections of fir trees, perhaps 15ft to 20ft high, set into the ground in lines about 40 yards apart. This was a replica of what we should find in the fields selected for our descent into France, i.e. fields sown with 'Rommel's Asparagus', as the anti-glider poles came to be called. Paratroop engineers would go down first and blow-up lines of these poles, a process which, because of their methodical Teutonic arrangement, would reveal lanes about 80 yards wide. Into such an area we were being trained to land in the dark.[7]

Further evidence of the imminence of D-Day came in another form. We were fitted out with escape kit. This consisted of ingenious items such as maps of Northern Europe printed on silk which could be folded small and concealed in our clothes, buttons which when unscrewed revealed a compass needle, ordinary-looking briar pipes with a compass in the stem, and, as standard issue to all of us, short pieces of hacksaw blade which had to be sewn into the seam of the fly of your trousers. Every soldier had a flat tin of a chocolate-type substance for use as an emergency ration which was said to be enough to keep one going for 48 hours. It could be eaten dry or mixed with water, and it was a military offence to broach it except in case of dire need.

There was known to be in France a tried and tested line of 'safe houses' and secret agents who would do their best to take you under their wing if you were put to evasion or escape. It had proved very effective in helping shot-down aircrew or escaped prisoners-of-war, and would no doubt assist us if we came down in the wrong place. There was one thing, however, which they were unable to provide and that was the passport-type photograph needed for a false identity card. Hence, we each had to carry pictures of ourselves wearing a nondescript civilian jacket. I could not help noticing when these were being taken how different and very ordinary the officers looked in 'civvies'. The uniform created the rank.

It was drilled into us that in the event of capture we should give away nothing under interrogation except 'name, rank and number'. About this time in the war it was realised that interrogation methods had become so refined that it was unrealistic for ordinary people to be expected to hold out to the last gasp, so the obligation to be heroic was replaced by a 'need to know' policy, whereby those at the bottom of the heap were told only the minimum necessary to do their immediate job. For this reason we did not know what the people outside our own flight were doing. It came as a surprise that it was our squadron which provided some of the pilots for the glider-borne assault on the River Orne and Orne Canal bridges on the east of the invasion area which was one of the earliest episodes, if not the earliest, of the whole D-Day operation, and one of the most remarkable feats of precision landing ever achieved.

Security was undoubtedly one of the successes of the war. Although the continuous bombardment of propaganda by means of films, lectures, leaflets and posters – the whole country was placarded with exhortations like 'Careless talk costs lives' and the more light-hearted 'Be like Dad, keep Mum' – turned security into a national obsession, there is no doubt that the invasion, when it did come, as to both place and time proved to be a complete surprise to the enemy, for which we who took part had reason to give thanks.

Knowing now what we were going to have to do, the where and the when quickly followed. It was shortly after the last 'strip' exercise on 28 May that we were bundled into lorries and conveyed to the middle of a wood. Not even approximately did we know where it was; it was probably somewhere in Hampshire. In the wood was a closely guarded camp, surrounded by barbed-wire entanglements and patrolled by military police. No one unauthorised could get in and we certainly could not get out. We were accommodated in tents. How many days we stayed there I cannot remember, except that one of them was my twenty-eighth birthday, to honour which my nearest and dearest had sent me a fine cake (made at considerable sacrifice of strictly rationed materials) which I ceremoniously cut with a fighting knife.

One morning we were taken down to a series of huts, also within the wooded camp. Here all was disclosed. A large map on the wall showed the beaches of Normandy and our approach-route to them. More impressive, and indeed quite astonishing, was a large-scale model of the eastern end of the invasion area, complete in every detail down to individual houses and trees. We were shown, not once but repeatedly, how and where we should land. But this was only part of it. There were photographs from all different heights and angles, showing our LZ in every detail, including our assigned meadow clearly sown with anti-glider obstacles. Above all was a cinematic film giving a pilot's eye view of our exact run-in, firstly by day and then in simulated night.

We were now in possession of one of the most vital secrets of the war: where the Allies would invade Europe. I remember the exalted feeling of being now among the elect. Of course we had been enjoined to complete secrecy under threat of unimaginable penalties. But that was not needed. I can only compare the sensation to one of consecration, such as when, as an impressionable adolescent, I had just been confirmed by the bishop and was awaiting my first communion.

We were kept in the camp until the day and hour had been fixed. As is well-known, General Eisenhower had had to postpone the start of the operation by twenty-four hours because of unfavourable weather. My next memory is of being in a vast hall at Brize Norton filled with aircrew and glider pilots. We were now told who would be towing us (my tug-pilot's name was Flight Lieutenant Horn, a New Zealander) and what course we would be flying. The take-off was somewhere around 0100 hours. The wing commander wound up his briefing by saying 'Then you will come back and we shall have eggs and bacon waiting for you.' Not for us, I thought.

That afternoon we had met our 'load'. Mine was unusual: a three-ton bulldozer with its driver from the Royal Engineers. This was one of two machines intended to roll the felled logs and other debris off the LZ in anticipation of the arrival of the 'second lift'. Loading was not easy. The bulldozer had to be driven up steel ramps on to the let-down portion of the glider's fuselage which served as a loading platform, slewed round, and fitted into the hold where it was firmly braced to the floor.[8]

It was pitch dark when we were bussed out to the line of gliders already connected up to the tugs. At the last moment a paratroop sergeant presented himself. He had damaged his shoulder on a practice drop, was unfit to jump, and, not wanting to be left behind whilst his unit was in action, had opted to come with us. For a paratrooper to ask to fly in a glider took a great deal of determination.

As we rolled down the runway we could dimly discern in the runway lights that the whole station had stayed up to wave us off. Among them was the son of a Hitchin friend of mine who was an RAF electrician on the station. About a month later he was best man at my wedding. The first leg of the course took us northwards into the East Midlands. We soon settled down to the familiar routine, with Jim and I taking the controls turn and turn about. We still had the feeling of: this was it; this was for real; this was the supreme endeavour for which all that long and exacting training had prepared us.

I can't say I was particularly nervous. We were immensely confident that the invasion would be a success, we had been admirably briefed and equipped, and were aware that thousands of equally well-prepared people were heading in the same direction by air and by sea. The only unknown was what we should find when we got there.

We were not at first conscious of all the other glider-tug combinations in the air around us as we were in a long line, well spaced out. The centre of our interest was, as usual, the tug in front. Otherwise all was dark. Presently we turned south and became more aware of aircraft alongside, above or below us. We must have been somewhere towards the west of London when we saw, away to our right, that the air was now filled with hundreds upon hundreds of bright red lights, which I can only compare to a long-drawn-out swarm of crimson bees. It was about the most remarkable sight I have ever witnessed. The lights were the port-side lights of the enormous air armada then marshalling, as we were, before setting course out across the English Channel. To us they seemed stationary in the air. As our angle to them changed, so did the lights change from red to white to green, or simply from red to green. Other streams of lights came into view. To the west the sky was full of them.

The moon must now have been rising and we could just glimpse the bald tops of the South Downs as we passed over them. My thoughts went to the folk sleeping down below in their darkened houses, and there flashed through my mind (as I am sure they did through the mind of many others that night) the lines from Henry V:

And gentlemen in England now a-bed
Shall think themselves accurs'd they were not here,
And hold their manhoods cheap, whiles any speaks
That fought with us upon Saint Crispin's Day.

The sense of history, of playing a not insignificant part in a great historical occasion, was upon me. Not for the first time was Britain going to the rescue of the continent of Europe.

Now came the 'moment of truth', or rather of a new reality. We dimly saw the line of the coast disappear beneath us and we were heading off into the dark. The tug told us, rather apologetically, that he was switching off his lights, so there was nothing to be seen except the glint of the moonlight on the wings of the tug which had been painted with broad white stripes to reduce the chance of mistaken attack by our own side – something which had happened at Sicily.[9] I was down in low-tow and supplementing the glimpses of the tug with the feel of the slip-stream and from what I could gather from the despised 'angle of dangle'.

It is well known that the weather on D-Day was far from ideal. Over the Channel there was a lot of cloud and though the flight lieutenant did his best to keep out of it, he could not do so entirely. We kept going in and out of the murk but I managed to keep station (at the later de-briefing Flight Lieutenant Horn said some kind things about this). When my turn came I attributed it to some steady flying on his part, an exchange of compliments which caused some amusement. We eventually ran into some thick cloud and stayed there for longer than I would have liked, when suddenly we came out of it. I knew immediately where we were. There below us, like a badly shaped question mark, was the mouth of the River Orne and the neighbouring canal, exactly as I had expected to find them. Further down into France, quite a way off (actually about 6 miles), was the blinking red light of the lead-in beacon positioned by the paratroops to mark our LZ.

As we had approached the coast there had been some flak coming up, by which we learned later one of our tugs had been shot down, and some accounts say it was intense. However, my mind was on something else and that was to get down with the least delay, and I was not unduly bothered about it. Our gliding approach required us to half-circle the beacon, and before we got there I began putting on flap as we were very much too high. I dived, with Jim, whose duty it was to keep an eye on the instruments, shouting that we were going too fast, at 100mph – enough to tear the flaps off.

I seemed to sense rather than see the ground coming up, and at the right moment levelled off and put her down. Once touched, she stayed on her wheels and came to a stop undamaged.

We had expected that all hell would break loose when we landed, but it did not. In fact when, after a very brief pause to catch our breath, we tumbled out, we were in mortal dread not of the enemy but of the other gliders. They were landing all over the place, some with spot-lights on, which was a dead give-away, others approaching from the wrong direction, and many crashing into the posts or other gliders. All this happened within the space of about a minute. When it was all over there was a sudden silence. All that could be heard was the gentle sighing of the wind through the grasses. Typically English I suppose, but the first thing we did in Normandy was to get out the large Thermos flasks and have a mug of tea.

The paratroop sergeant who, forgotten by me, had been sitting by himself at the back, now made his appearance. Far from thanking me for having got him into France all in one piece, he left us with scant courtesy, merely remarking that the landing had been a bit rough, as indeed it had. With that he just disappeared.[10]

The next problem was to get the bulldozer out. We let down the hinged portion of the fuselage and put props underneath. From this platform to the ground was about four feet and sloping from it we fixed the steel ramps via which the bulldozer was intended to descend. Unfortunately it didn't. The ramps were shaped like troughs and the bulldozer's tracks had no sooner entered them than they stuck fast. The machine could go neither forward or back, no matter how hard and ingeniously we and the driver tried.

There are occasions when a resort is justified to brute force and bloody ignorance. I summoned a jeep which happened to be passing by, coupled it up with ropes to the two props, and with a jerk down came platform, troughs, bulldozer and all. The tough little machine was undamaged and 'within an hour of landing' as *By Air to Battle* puts it, it was merrily working away among the debris.[11] With the disregard for inconvenient facts and preference for simple explanations which seems to be the hallmark of wartime journalism, it is reported that the bulldozer 'broke through the floor of the glider'. Given the immense strength of the Horsa, particularly as to the part of it which supported the load, it is difficult to imagine how it was thought that this could have been achieved.

It had been quite dark at the moment of landing, but now the pre-dawn light was coming up. Shouldering our rifles, bandoliers of ammunition and other kit, we gravitated towards the southern end of the sweep of meadowland which formed our LZ (in 1988 it was much the same as it was in 1944, except at that time it was down to grass). There we found the church of Ranville at the top of a slight slope and the village beyond. This, though we did not know it at the time, was the first village in France to be liberated.

Among ourselves the main question was, who had come down safely and who was missing? So far as we could see, nearly all our flight were present. However, there was one first pilot sitting on a bank, clearly in a state of clinical shock. Where, we asked, was Jock Beveridge, his second pilot? All he could say was that in the process of landing Jock had been there one minute and was gone the next. The glider had flown straight into one of the anti-glider obstacles which had gouged Jock out of the cockpit, leaving the first pilot untouched. Where Jock was now he did not know.

We were gathered around the entrance gates of a small chateau to the east of the village. There was no particular hurry or sense of urgency, no one was barking orders or doing anything dramatic. Regardless of the fact that we were probably the most easterly of all troop formations in the bridgehead (though a variety of other troops were scattered about beyond us, the River Dives having been mistaken for the Orne in some cases; of course we did not know this at the time) and therefore in line for the expected counter-attack, it was all very low-key. Our role was now to defend the two bridges and, more immediately, to protect the chateau which had been taken over as the Command HQ for the area.

It was by now almost fully light. There were noises of shots going off and shells falling, but these did not build up into a concerted attack. Now and again we heard heavy thunderous rumbles where saturation bombing or shelling from warships was destroying enemy fortifications on the coast. We were placed under the command of a staff sergeant, a stranger to us. He told Jim and me to go forward to the edge of some trees and dig ourselves in, whilst he settled himself comfortably and out of sight behind one of the pillars of the gate. I came across this 'you go out front and I'll be here right behind you' syndrome again later.

We watched the road running across fields to woods half a mile distant from which we expected to see the enemy burst at any minute. Nothing happened. Later we were repositioned in an orchard and had to dig another slit trench (digging slit-trenches with our entrenching tools became an all-too-frequent activity) facing the same field.

There was now rather more shot and shell coming over, but it was high up and not specifically directed at us. As I lay prone in my slit-trench, a shallow one because of rocks underneath, I heard a shell burst and pieces of metal began to whizz around. To make myself less conspicuous and also to provide a rest for my rifle, I had placed my haversack on the edge of the trench in front of me. I could hear a shell fragment humming down from a height above me. It hit my haversack about a foot forward of my head, cutting the canvas and denting my mess-tin. The jagged metal weighed six or eight ounces and was too hot to touch. I kept it for a year or two.

There was another incident there. A girl having milked the cows – the work of a farm goes on whether there is an invasion or not – she gave us some of the thick brown Normandy milk, and Jim said there was nothing he wanted more than a nice cup of tea. Our ration-pack was a miracle of compression with blocks and slabs of vitamin-charged compositions, oatmeal, tea and meat among them. I 'brewed up' on our little hob heated by solidified methylated spirits, and duly made the tea. I gave Jim his mug, he took a long pull, and spat the mixture out: I had made the tea with the meat-cube. Never have I known anyone more disgusted with me, nor for a better reason, than Jim was that morning. I failed to convince him that the enriched protein combined with the full-cream milk gave him a more nutritious drink than any he would ever have again.

Later we were gathered further back under a hedgerow (digging yet another slit-trench of course), when in the late morning or early afternoon we perceived activity on the north or Channel side of the LZ, and this was the relief which, with no great anxiety, we had been waiting for. Memory is fallible and much coloured by what one has subsequently heard or read, but I really believe we heard the bagpipes of the Lovat Scouts as they came jauntily up from the beach, passed through our positions (such as they were) and moved on.[12] There was now nothing further for us to do. We saw no sign of the enemy, though shots were going off and bullets whistling over, and I have since read that several sharp engagements took place around the chateau and that some of our men ambushed a tank.

Sometime during that day (this was indeed 'The Longest Day', as one of the accounts of it has been called) the Padre, who was with us all the way from Africa to Arnhem, where he stayed behind to tend the wounded, asked Jim and me to go with him to try to find out what had happened to Jock Beveridge.

We walked down into the LZ where there were gliders at all angles, some much damaged, others surprisingly not, but more widely spaced apart than I had expected. Fortunately for ourselves the area had by no means been fully sown with the anti-glider obstacles, though there were lines of pot-holes which had been dug, though the poles had not been installed. (There was a story, probably true, that the man employed by the Germans to dig the holes applied to the Army 'for his payment for work done', and was very aggrieved that it was not forthcoming. Presumably one Army was as good as another from his point of view.)

We found the glider and followed its tracks backwards through the grass. Sure enough we came across what looked like a bundle of thrown-away clothes. Jock's body was badly broken up. His arm was fractured, his wrist-watch smashed. There was not much visible blood. The top of his skull had been completely taken off, like the top of an egg, and one could see the channels of the blood-vessels on the inner side of the bone. Jock had been a compulsive talker and the irrational notion went through my mind, 'so that's what made Jock tick!' The Padre gently pulled up the camouflage scarf we all wore round our necks and reverently covered what was left of Jock's face. He was the first dead man we saw, and probably the first glider pilot killed in this part of the operation. He lies in Ranville cemetery. I have seen his grave.

There were other casualties, caused by random shots which kept whipping across the area. One man got hit in the upper chest and though there was not much outward sign of damage, he was said to have died later in the casualty station set up in Ranville church.[13]

Another case was so extraordinary that I should not have believed it had I not had it from the man himself. Some friends noticed a small hole in one side of T's helmet (the round airborne variety which made us look like medieval men-at arms) and exclaimed 'T, you've been hit!' Walking round to the other side, sure enough, there was the exit hole. 'T' was persuaded to go to the casualty station where it was confirmed that indeed a high-velocity missile had penetrated right through what were then known as the 'silent areas' of the brain's frontal lobes. He himself had had no knowledge or sensation of this. Though outwardly normal, there was something odd about him, and I heard that later on he had, or feigned he had, bouts of amnesia, and that some of these were not unconnected with an effort to free himself from an unsatisfactory marriage. What the truth of it all was I never knew, our life being one of continual comings and goings. Very strange things happen in war.[14]

Late that evening the 'second lift' came in. Heralded by a sudden violent barrage of anti-aircraft fire, the air was filled with tugs and gliders, the latter swooping towards our LZ, the former dropping their trailing ropes and beating a rapid retreat. The pandemonium lasted no more than two or three minutes, then, just as suddenly, things were back to normal again.[15]

We spent the night in the open air and it passed without incident. The next morning we were assembled in flights and marched down to the beach.

One of the effects of memory is that it is defective about distance and in my recollection our march that day was just a short stroll. In reality it must have been a trek of 12 miles or more. We passed over the two bridges, noting with a professional eye the precision with which our comrades had put their gliders down within a stone's throw of their objectives. The famous café, the first building to be liberated, we did not specially notice: it was not famous until later.[16] We walked through the village streets, in which some damage and a few corpses told of the fight that had taken place, until we came to a crossroads where we stopped. There was a German rifleman in a church tower shooting at people; he had already killed several members of the Military Police directing the now considerable traffic. A tank was engaged in blowing the top off the church and the rifleman with it.

We continued our march single-file at the side of the road, with all manner of men and materials coming up from the beach. Some of the men mocked us: 'You're going the wrong way, mates.' Others replied 'They've done their part.' In one village prisoners were being assembled and marched away. One as he went turned and waved to a woman in a house door who waved sadly back to him, her lover perhaps, or even her husband. I wondered what would happen to her afterwards; female collaborators had their hair shaved off. In the grass verge beyond the village lay a fine-looking, smartly turned out, young German soldier, his chest shot away by a burst of machine-gun fire, part of the waste of war.

As we approached the beach and could glimpse the ships, a Focke-Wolf suddenly appeared from the low cloud, dropped a huge egg-shaped bomb, and flew off. From nowhere a Spitfire swooped after it, and the next thing we saw was a parachute drifting down. It all happened in less time than it takes to tell.

The beach, all things considered, was remarkably tidy. Some disabled landing-craft were washing about in the surf and there was other wreckage. However, round the bastions of the sea wall were what looked like piled-up stores under canvas sheets. They were indeed piled up, but they were not stores but the bodies of men who had fallen in the first assault. I noticed a wax-like hand sticking out. It had on it a wedding ring, token of some poor woman back home who did not know, and would not know for some time, that she was a widow.

In the desultory way in which such things always seemed to happen, a landing-craft came in, took us aboard and ferried us out to a mother-ship a mile or so offshore. There were other craft dotted about as far as the eye could see. We were put below in a cabin full of bunk beds and given a can of self-heating soup. The tins had a tube down the centre containing some material – we understood that it was gun-cotton – which when lit smouldered downwards and heated the soup around it nearly to boiling point. Thus refreshed we went to bed. Later we were woken by an enormous shindy as the Germans tried to bomb us and the fleet replied. The bombs, though near, missed us. Very tired we dozed off. In the morning the ship sailed and put us ashore, I never knew exactly where, but believe it was Seaford. After an interminable delay which we spent sitting in someone's front garden, lorries came and took us back to Brize Norton.

I suppose we all thought a good deal of ourselves after this. We had taken a daring and unique part in one of the biggest military operations in history – and we had been successful in it. We all walked six inches taller as a result. In retrospect this pride was unfortunate. It gave us and our higher command a false sense of insuperability. How grievously we would pay for it was to be seen later.

Early days with the Royal Army Service Corps (RASC). Robert Ashby (standing, fourth from right) on a motor mechanics course, Norwich, 1940. (*R. Ashby Collection*)

'Total Soldiers' – Elementary Flying Training School, 1942. Robert Ashby is in the middle row, standing, seventh from the left. (*R. Ashby Collection*)

'Ready for Action'. Staff Sergeant Robert Ashby, Glider Pilot Regiment. (*R. Ashby Collection*)

A Horsa glider in training. Note the extended flaps for landing. (*R. Ashby Collection*)

A Horsa AS.51 being towed into position for take-off. (*IWM CH10356*)

General Aircraft Hotspur glider, used extensively to train glider pilots. (*Public Domain*)

Glider pilots in smocks and battledress. (*IWM H040984*)

D-Day. Tugs and gliders take off from RAF Tarrant Rushton. Note the D-Day markings. *(IWM CL000026)*

Sergeant Jim Donaldson, Ashby's second pilot during glider operations, training with Tiger Moths at Shrewton airfield. (*R. Ashby Collection*)

'Rommel's Asparagus'. German defenders often 'planted' large open fields near strategic targets with poles to rip apart Allied gliders as they landed. The poles were often wired together to effect a cheese-cutting action on the wood and canvas fuselages. (*Public Domain*)

A restored 3-ton Clarkair bulldozer. A similar model was delivered by Robert Ashby's Horsa glider on D-Day to enable the landing zones to be cleared of debris. These bulldozers were normally carried in the larger Hamilcar gliders. Ashby encountered some difficulty in the unloading of the machine. (*Public Domain*)

D-Day. Operation Tonga and Pegasus bridge. Three gliders, containing men of the 6th Airlanding Brigade, land south of the bridge. The top glider contained Major John Howard. (*IWM MH002074*)

On their wedding day in 1944: Robert Ashby and his bride Jeane.
(*R. Ashby Collection*)

Tug towing a Horsa glider. Towing speeds could reach more than 150mph.
(*R. Ashby Collection*)

Arnhem, September 1944. The road bridge showing knocked-out German armoured vehicles, destroyed by Lieutenant Colonel John Frost and the men of 2 PARA. (IWM MH002061)

Arnhem. Airborne troops dig in near the Oosterbeek perimeter. (*IWM BU001167*)

Arnhem. An anti-tank unit from the 1st Border Regiment firing a 6-pdr gun, recently delivered by a Horsa glider. As this photograph was taken, the gun, nicknamed 'Gallipoli', engaged a German *Flammpanzer* tank and destroyed it. (*IWM BU001109*)

A PIAT anti-tank weapon in action with its two-man team – a weapon commonly used by glider pilots at Arnhem. (*Library and Archives of Canada PA-114595*)

Arnhem. *Generalmajor* Friedrich Kussin, commander of German forces in Arnhem, lies dead in his car after being ambushed by 3 PARA, 17 September 1944. (*IWM BU001155*)

Arnhem. Two sergeants from the Glider Pilot Regiment search ruins in Oosterbeek. (*IWM BU001100*)

DUKW amphibious vehicles being unloaded. Expected to assist in the river evacuation at the end of the Battle of Arnhem, the DUKWs were withdrawn at the last minute when someone realised the Lower Rhine river banks were too steep. (*Public Domain*)

An M22 Locust light tank disembarking from a General Aircraft Hamilcar glider. One such combination exploded in mid-air during Operation Varsity – an incident referred to by Robert Ashby. (*Public Domain*)

Operation Varsity. Hamilcar and Horsa gliders and their Halifax tugs prepare for take-off from RAF Woodbridge, March 1945. *(IWM CH014882)*

Loading a jeep into a Horsa. Fuel carried in vehicles was a frequent cause of combustion in flight or on landing. (*Public domain*)

Crossing the Rhine. US troops crossing under fire. (*NARA 208-YE-132*)

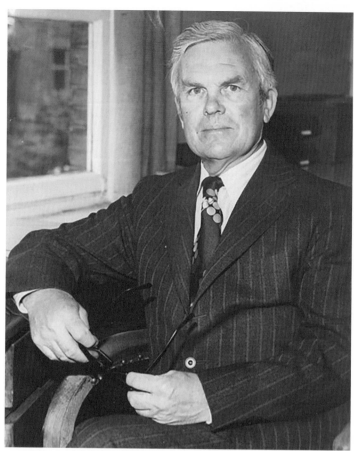

Surrey County Librarian.
(*R. Ashby Collection*)

Robert Ashby celebrates his
100th birthday with four
generations of his family.
(*Kate Shemilt*)

Chapter 10

After D-Day

The reason why we precious people had been withdrawn so promptly from Normandy was the expectation that we should soon be wanted again. The British part of the airborne operations had been carried out by the 6th Airborne Division, to which we had been attached *pro tem*, and there was still the 1st Airborne ready and waiting. We filled in time at Shrewton, a small informal grass airfield on the western side of Salisbury Plain, at Leicester East, and elsewhere. There was no sign of another operation being prepared for us, and in the interim I got married.

Although this is a record of my military and not of my private life, the two overlap here in a curious way which is perhaps relevant. For my wedding I was given forty-eight hours leave, from Friday to Sunday. A friend flew me from Shrewton to Denham airfield, from which I hitched to Watford. The wedding was in Hitchin and the only honeymoon hotel my bride could find was the George and Dragon at Baldock. Sitting in the train at Hitchin station on Sunday afternoon with my young wife being escorted away in tears by a friend, I thought the train seemed to take a long time to get started, when someone raced along the platform asking for Staff Sergeant Ashby. The Army had extended my leave for a whole week, and my sister, having received the news at Watford, had frantically phoned round all likely places. The message thus reached me in the nick of time. An astounded wife and friend heard the pounding of my army boots as I raced up the road behind them.

The extra leave, though obviously welcome, brought with it a difficulty: it was almost impossible in that fifth year in the war, to make arrangements to stay anywhere. After burdening first our Hitchin friend and then my parents at Watford, we managed to get some days in the annexe of a small hotel at Boscombe, full of long-term residents who had sat out the war. Up to then the whole of the south coast had been closed to visitors.

By the end of August there was still no sign of another op. The records say that no fewer than fifteen were planned for us, but of these we knew nothing except for one where we were put into immediate readiness.[1] It happened like this.

One of the ways in which unusual formations like us were trained was with 'initiative exercises'. Men were sent out, usually in pairs, to travel considerable distances with the instruction to 'live off the land' and to spend no more than half-a-crown, an amount which at that time would just about pay for a modest meal at a working-class restaurant. The accomplishment of the assignment was to be proved (unless a rendezvous was fixed) by bringing back something like a station-master's stamp or the name of a village pub, though it is on record that two of our men collected the signature of Queen Mary![2]

In our case – and it seems an odd thing to do with troops who might be wanted at very short notice – we were sent off on a Friday and told to report in at Aberystwyth the following Tuesday evening. Naturally everyone went off home, including Jim and I to my parents at Watford.

Starting out on Monday morning, we succeeded that night in reaching Welshpool, where we asked the police inspector if we could sleep in the cells. However, he had a better idea and gave us bed and breakfast in his house. Arrived at Aber, and having spent the night on a hillside in the rain (in sleeping bags designed for just that purpose), we were suddenly entrained back to where we had come from.

This was about the most unpleasant journey I have ever made. Joining the main line somewhere near Birmingham I suppose, we were packed into an over-crowded pitch-dark train, where there was scarcely room even to stand in the corridor. One rash soldier, not one of ours, had his face crushed by an army boot when he tried to lie down on the floor. In our suffocating carriage a civilian kept grotesquely saying 'Go on, kick my shins', apparently having artificial legs. After an entirely sleepless night we ended up at Greenham Common, Newbury, the scene later of the famous women's anti-nuclear protest.

The operation must have been imminent because we were briefed for it. It was to be an airborne assault on the palace of Rambouillet, near Paris. I rather fancied the chance of landing in the grounds of a stately home complete with ornamental lakes and fountains. It was not to be, however. Operation Transfigure was postponed, then scrubbed, the ground forces in France having got there first. This was somewhere between 13 and 17 August.[3] After filling in time with some cross-country flights at Hampstead Norris, we were taken back to Brize Norton in early September 1944.

The accounts of this period tell of the bad effect on morale created by this seemingly pointless waiting. My own recollection is that we were, personally, ready to go, and often discussed among ourselves the various ways in which we thought we ought to be used in speeding the advance through France, which was apparently sweeping all before it. But we were not kept at readiness, not 'like greyhounds in the slips, straining upon the start'. We had been so keyed up for the immense effort of D-Day that, as athletes do, we had lost a certain amount of 'form' after it. In any case the war was well on the way to being won, another push (in which it was assumed we would take some part) and it would be all over.

How wrong we were we soon found out – at Arnhem.

Chapter 11

Arnhem

By the end of August 1944 German forces had finally been defeated in Normandy, and Paris was liberated. In the next few weeks US, British and Canadian forces swept up through Belgium, poised to advance into Holland and then into Germany. But an early end to the war was far from assured. For not only had the Allies to resolve the difficulty of keeping long lines of communication open, but they also had to keep their rapidly advancing columns supplied with fuel. Meanwhile, the retreating German forces had managed to strengthen their resolve and coupled with new drafts of men from Army and Luftwaffe units, promised stiff resistance in Holland.[1]

Eisenhower now favoured a broad frontal attack on Germany, but the commander of 21st Army Group, the newly promoted Field Marshal Bernard Montgomery, proposed a single thrust through Holland that would outflank the Siegfried Line, encircle the industrial Ruhr and pave the way for the final drive towards Berlin. However, there were significant problems with this proposal. The German Army now had the advantage of much shorter lines of communication than the Allies and although the British Second Army captured Antwerp on 4 September, Montgomery had failed to secure the adjacent Scheldt estuary and islands. Consequently, German coastal batteries continued to make the port unusable and yet it was vital for any Allied push into Germany that supplies and ammunition could be brought in through Antwerp.

Nevertheless, Montgomery, who was desperate to be the first Allied commander to cross the Rhine, continued to press his plan with Eisenhower. To clear a route for the advance of the British XXX Corps, he argued that US, British and Polish airborne forces could be dropped ahead to capture nine bridges up to and including the road bridge and rail bridge over the Lower Rhine at Arnhem. Once the river crossings were secured, Allied motorised and armoured forces would swiftly advance over this 'carpet', effectively creating a salient into enemy territory. From this salient the Allies would

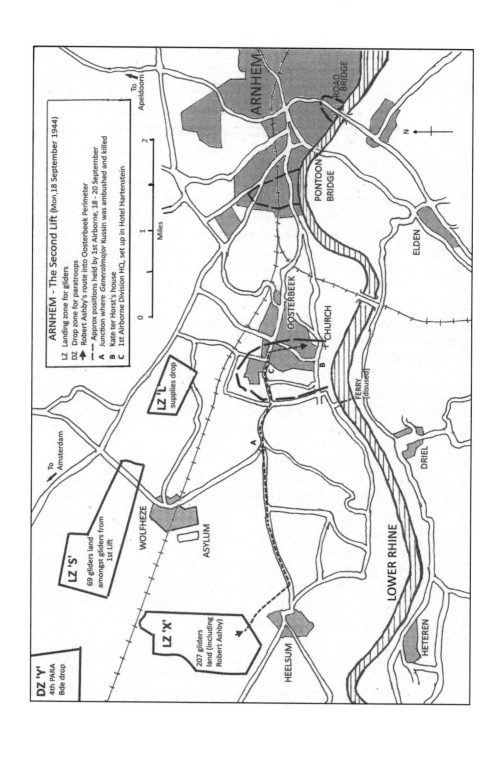

ARNHEM – The Second Lift (Mon, 18 September 1944)

LZ   Landing zone for gliders
DZ   Drop zone for paratroops
   Robert Ashby's route into Oosterbeek Perimeter
–   Approx positions held by 1st Airborne, 18 – 20 September
A   Junction where *Generalmajor* Kussin was ambushed and killed
B   Kate ter Horst's house
C   1st Airborne Division HQ, set up in Hotel Hartenstein

To Apeldoorn

ARNHEM

ROAD BRIDGE

PONTOON BRIDGE

ELDEN

OOSTERBEEK

† CHURCH

FERRY [disused]

DRIEL

LOWER RHINE

HETEREN

Miles
0   1   2

N

To Amsterdam

DZ 'Y'
4th PARA
Bde drop

LZ 'S'
69 gliders land
amongst gliders from
1st Lift

WOLFHEZE

ASYLUM

LZ 'X'
207 gliders
land (including
Robert Ashby)

HEELSUM

LZ 'L'
supplies drop

launch a three-pronged attack. On the left flank they could move westwards towards The Hague, from where the new V2 rocket attacks were being launched. Apart from reducing this threat, the thrust would also cut off German forces in the Scheldt and relieve the pressure on Antwerp. The central prong of the advance would take the Allies into Germany, while on the right flank they could advance into the Ruhr, the industrial heartland of Germany.

It was a bold but reckless plan, which ignored the difficulties of the terrain and therefore the speed at which land forces could reach and reinforce the airborne troops at the very head of the advance at Arnhem. The 'carpet' was in fact a central highway with often boggy ground on either side, which meant that frequent armour or vehicle breakdowns could cause blockages, hampering the advancing columns. Unheeded intelligence reports on the strength of enemy forces, together with the limitations of wireless communications would just serve to compound the problems.

The operation was named Market Garden. The airborne part of the plan, which involved the capture and holding of the bridges, was called 'Market' and the simultaneous ground assault by Lieutenant General Horrocks' XXX Corps, to advance and join up with the airborne forces, was named 'Garden'. It would require a considerable air armada, involving 34,000 US and British troops, including over 11,000 who would be deployed at Arnhem.

The US 82nd and 101st Airborne Divisions were to tackle the nearer bridges, including at Eindhoven and Nijmegen, while elements of I British Airborne Corps (Lieutenant General 'Boy' Browning) were to be deployed at Arnhem. Browning had at his disposal the 1st British Airborne Division (Major General Roy Urquhart), which included the 1st and 4th Parachute Brigades as well as the 1st Airlanding Brigade comprising infantry battalions trained to be delivered by gliders. The Glider Pilot Regiment itself was attached to the division and the long-awaited deployment of the Polish 1st Independent Parachute Brigade (Major General Stanisław Sosabowski) promised to strengthen the airborne mission. In addition to these airborne troops, the landings would include sappers, signallers and field gunners together with their equipment, vehicles and guns.

However, despite the quality of this force, Operation Market was fraught with danger. The recent glider disasters in the assault on Sicily persuaded the planners that only daytime operations were feasible. Because of the scale of the whole operation, some 3,500 aircraft were required to deliver the troops, weapons and supplies. However, these were simply not available, at least not for one lift, so not only were the numbers of aircraft insufficient for the British 1st Airborne Division, but those available would have to be allocated over three lifts on successive days. It took little imagination to see that after the first drop the enemy would be alerted and could repulse any successive lifts. Furthermore, anticipated heavy German flak nearer the bridge ruled out a closer landing to the road bridge, so the only suitable landing sites were some 7 miles west of the target.

On Sunday, 17 September 1944 (Day One) the first lift took off for Arnhem. Some 321 gliders, towed by RAF aircraft, delivered airborne and airlanding troops, together with 17-pounder anti-tank guns and towing vehicles, Bren-gun carriers, jeeps and support weapons.[2] The Horsas carried troops, jeeps and 6-pounder guns, while the thirteen heavier Hamilcar gliders would carry the 17-pounder guns, 75mm howitzers and their heavy tractor transports.

Robert Ashby took part in the second lift on Monday, 18 September (Day Two), which saw a further 276 gliders (257 Horsas, 15 Hamilcars and 4 Hadrians) successfully deliver more vehicles, artillery, the remaining divisional HQ personnel, together with the last of the airlanding troops. This was followed by waves of C-47 Dakotas carrying 'sticks' of paratroopers, while Stirlings dropped supplies.[3]

The third lift on Day Three involved a further thirty-five Horsa gliders and a Hamilcar, brought in to reinforce the anti-tank squadrons, but enemy small arms and mortar fire wreaked terrible havoc amongst the gliders coming into land. Unfortunately, friendly fire further compounded the misery of those trying to disembark, while ack-ack fire ripped through circling Dakotas and Stirlings trying to drop supplies. Indeed, the mission for these transport planes was grim. In the days after the initial surprise of the assault, German 88mm guns were prepared for further British aircraft formations and greeted them with a wall of flak. The RAF crews returned again and again to run the gauntlet and drop supplies, most of which would fall into enemy hands.[4]

After the initial landing, and utilising the surviving jeeps, the division's reconnaissance squadron spearheaded the advance along the road, north of the Neder Rijn (Lower Rhine). They were joined by the 2nd Parachute Battalion, commanded by Lieutenant Colonel John Frost, tasked with capturing both the railway and road bridge over the river. They found the railway bridge already blown but moved on to secure the northern approaches of the road bridge. Meanwhile SS units blocked the advance of the 1st and 3rd Parachute Battalions and pinned them down in the suburb of Ooster-beek. Frost and his men were isolated and over the following days fought an heroic action to hold on to their shrinking territory around the bridgehead. Further lifts of British airborne forces continued to arrive, but tough German resistance bottled them up within their perimeter in Oosterbeek. The intensity of the fighting varied within the perimeter. Towards the northern part, around the crossroads near the 1st Airborne Division HQ and the temporary dressing stations, the enemy concentrated more firepower. In the southern area of the perimeter, towards the Neder Rijn, where Robert Ashby spent most of his time, enemy pressure appeared to be lighter. Glider pilots who had advanced beyond Oosterbeek and then retreated back into the perimeter found themselves defending the divisional HQ, which had been set up in the large hotel that ironically had previously housed the German regional HQ. The pilots were dug-in across numerous slit trenches in the hotel grounds and suffered repeated mortar bombardments. Radio com-munications, always a problem during the war, proved extremely difficult at Arnhem and cohesion between units was further compromised when Major General Urquhart left his divisional HQ to go forward, after com-munications had failed, to assess the front line and was cut-off from his staff for three critical days.

Among the diaries and memoirs of Arnhem combatants, many testify to the conduct of the German soldiers. They adhered to the Geneva Conven-tion and there are only rare instances of them deliberately firing on Red Cross teams retrieving the wounded – all the more surprising considering the high number of SS forces involved.

When fresh supplies landed in enemy territory it was dispiriting to the men on the ground, since many had lost their rucksacks during rapid house evacuations, but at least there were provisions and tinned food left by Dutch inhabitants. Despite their losses during the fighting, the vast bulk of the local Dutch population were in favour of liberation, though the Allied force could not count on much material support from the Dutch Resistance. Their cells were lightly armed and although their intelligence could prove useful, they had been subject to enemy penetration. There were also a number of local members of the Dutch National Socialist Party, who either fled at the beginning or stayed to continue their collaboration with the Germans.

Lieutenant Colonel John Frost and his band of lightly armed Paras succeeded in taking the northern end of the bridge and heroically held off repeated German armoured assaults. After several days enemy artillery started to pound his position with phosphorus shells, and without supplies of water his men were powerless to put out the resulting fires. Even the much-delayed drop of 1,000 men of the Polish Independent Parachute Brigade failed to turn the situation. They landed south of the river, opposite near Driel, and despite heroic attempts to reach the Oosterbeek perimeter, only 150 men succeeded. With no sign of relief from XXX Corps, the decision was made to withdraw all airborne forces. Those who were physically able, retreated south across the river, while British artillery, further south near Nijmegen, gave covering fire.

Ultimately, British airborne forces were dropped too far in advance of approaching land forces and too deep into enemy territory. The shortage of aircraft meant that airborne lifts had to be spread over three days, and supplies were similarly extended. Robert Ashby gives a damning indictment of the lack of command and control on the ground, a factor which must have contributed to the high casualties. Of the nearly 12,000 men who took part in the Arnhem operation, it has been estimated that 1,485 were killed and 6,525 became prisoners of war. Although the 1st British Airborne Division was decimated as a result, the Glider Pilot Regiment suffered the highest proportion of casualties, losing 229 killed and 469 wounded or captured out of a total of 1,262 glider pilots committed to the battle. Estimates of enemy dead exceed 1,750.[5]

* * *

Operation Market Garden started for me when, with Jim Donaldson as second pilot, I flew a Horsa from Brize Norton down to Manston aerodrome in Kent. I remember this flight very well because it took place on a golden early autumn afternoon in clear, still air with the sun throwing long shadows across the fields. We knew we were going on an operation but there was no unusual sense of apprehension. We assumed everything would be like D-Day: meticulous preparation, careful briefing, and every chance of a successful result.

Manston's main feature was a massive landing strip extending about halfway across the North Foreland on the easterly-most tip of Kent. As one of the airfields nearest to the continent it had had its full share of the war. Its shelters still containing rotted blankets which no one had had time to clear away told of how much they had been put to their vital use.

At the time of our brief stay Manston was still a fighter base. There were fighter pilots in the sergeants' mess informally garbed in RAF uniform supplemented by flying boots and brightly coloured scarves. It was this aerodrome, I believe, which had been the scene of a fuss during the Battle of Britain in September 1940 when a station commander had insisted that no one, not even the pilots due out on or just in from an operation, should enter the mess improperly dressed or expect meals at other than the regulation times – so inflexible was the Service mind at that time. There was nothing of this when we were there.

But the station's main use now seemed to be to act as a haven for disabled aircraft. One part of it was a graveyard of shot-up and crashed remains of many types of planes, some of them were as ancient as the old Fleet Air Arm string and canvas Swordfish, and others as modern as Flying Fortresses. We went into one of the latter. There were pools of dried-up blood and blood-soaked dressings on the floor and bullet holes in the fuselage.

Although the main thrust of the war in Europe had by now reached the Belgian-Dutch border and much of the ground and air effort had been moved to the continent, the bomber bases in England were still in active use. Thus aircraft unable to fly further were still homing in on Manston. The arrival of these was announced to the whole station by tannoy, so that everyone heard, for example, that a disabled Liberator was now on its way in. Sure enough, in a minute or two the gigantic plane could be seen lumbering slowly through the low cloud, one of its engines a red glow, another stopped. It made a circuit of the airfield, three or four parachutes blossomed out and the great machine came in at a flat angle to grate along the runway on its belly, throwing up sparks whilst fire trucks and ambulances rushed out to it. This sort of thing occurred several times while we were there.

We arrived at Manston on 7 September and for a while nothing happened. There was a general assumption that we would be going somewhere, but when and where no one knew. We just hung about. There was no preparation or training for what was to come, no honing of the razor, as it were. I remember no feeling of keenness to get into battle or of reluctance to do so. It was all very routine.

We were by no means confined to camp. By hitching lifts to London, I managed to get home once or twice. Such leave was informal though officially condoned. It was the practice to leave through a gap in a fence which gave on to a main road, thus avoiding the guardroom, and to return by an early newspaper train from an east London station – Fenchurch Street, I think – to which one walked through the blacked-out streets from the nearest available underground. Partings in the bleak pre-dawn hours, not knowing when the next meeting would be, were the worst aspect of this sort of jaunt.

One evening some of us were in a pub in Ramsgate when we fell into the company of a crew of a torpedo boat. The lieutenant in charge invited two of us to join him on a patrol the next night along the enemy-occupied coast. We should certainly have gone, but, telephoning the next day for confirmation of place and time, I learned that the sea was too rough for the boat to put out. I have since wondered what the upshot would have been had we got ourselves killed, wounded or captured in the sort of engagement these boats used to indulge in. It would have been an unusual form of absence without leave.

In view of the easy-going attitude which the above events illustrate, it comes as a surprise to read that Market Garden, the sixteenth operation to be set up after D-Day, was authorised on 10 September 1944, given a definite go-ahead on 12 September, and fixed for 17 September.[6] Thus, all the time we were doing nothing in particular, preparations were being made, of which not a glimmer percolated through to ourselves who were going to be a vital element in it.

As to the objective of Market Garden, readers who are interested in the course the war took will know of the controversy which arose at this time about the Allies' overall strategy. Our main armies now stood on the Dutch border, Brussels and Belgium having been liberated on 3 September.[7] General Montgomery favoured the idea of a rapier-like thrust northwards through Holland and wheeling round eastwards to cut off the Ruhr, Germany's industrial heartland, from the rest of the country. General Eisenhower, the commander-in-chief, with his mind on the immensely long lines of supply stretching back to Cherbourg, and also on public relations consideration, favoured a broad front approach to the Rhine, in which his subordinate generals, such as the flamboyant Patton, could be given equal chances of glory.

Montgomery and Eisenhower were not on good terms, and my private reading of what transpired is that the latter, wearied by Montgomery's importunity, said, whether to himself or to others, 'To Hell with him then; if he thinks he can do it, we'll just let him try!' The thrust was made without a proper assessment of the pros and cons, particularly the cons, without regard to the sort of terrain over which the airborne and the ground troops would have to fight, and with inadequate support on either flank. It was a gamble. If it had come off it would have been a major breakthrough, but it did not come off. It threw away, uselessly, one of the best divisions the British Army then had.

There were several bridges to the north of the starting line, but the major objectives were two vast spans, respectively over the Waal at Nijmegen and over the Lower Rhine at Arnhem, which was about 10 miles to the north of it. As the official account, *By Air to Battle*, has it, 'To the 1st Airborne Division fell the honour of taking the bridge at Arnhem' – that is one way of looking at it. The other bridges were assaulted from the south and from the sides; at Arnhem the decision was to put down the division on the northern bank of a wide and fast-flowing river.

I cannot remember precisely when we knew that the operation was definitely 'on', but it must have been Friday, 15 September or Saturday, 16 September. I had made a visit home on the previous Wednesday, and this illustrates a feature of airborne operations launched from Britain which made them more difficult than they might have been: one was in the peace and security of one's home one day and in the battle line a few days later. There was no time to adjust, to acclimatise to the conditions of warfare.

Weapons and ammunition were now issued. I was given a Sten gun, a pistol and, at the last moment, a PIAT. The pistol was a Smith and Wesson revolver. I was pleased to have this – pistols always gave status – but when I tried it out on the RAF indoor shooting range, which seemed a prudent thing to do before going into action, I found it frequently did not fire owing to some defect in the firing pin. As far as I knew there were no facilities to have it mended, so I did nothing about it. It is perhaps symptomatic of the frame of mind in which we went out, firstly that someone thought fit to issue a defective pistol, and, secondly, that I was not very worried about it. I suppose it did not enter my head that one day soon I might have to use it.[8]

The PIAT needs explanation. The full Army name was Projector Infantry Anti-Tank and it was officially described as a 'spigot mortar 0'. It was a cumbersome, not to say bizarre piece of equipment. Made of sheet metal, unlike the solid steel of our other weapons, it had an improvised look about it, as if manufactured in a back-street workshop for insurgent use. About 4ft long it consisted of a padded butt and a tubular body in which was accommodated a powerful spring, with a long trigger, almost a handle, sticking out below. The front end of the body had been formed into a trough like an open drainpipe into which one laid the bomb. This was spherical at the head with a hardened tip, whilst the tail was a tube with fins, about a foot long overall, containing at its upper end a propellant similar to a shotgun cartridge without the shot. The mortar had to be cocked by drawing back the spring. On pressing, or rather pulling, the trigger, which took some effort, a shaft of steel leapt out of the body and entered the tube of the bomb, detonating the cartridge which sent the bomb on its way. The considerable recoil was taken by the spring-loaded shaft and the shoulder of the operator. Because of the kick, the weapon could effectively be used only by lying prone behind it.

I was not overjoyed at being allocated this device. It was heavy and ungainly to carry, and we were already burdened with our other weapons and ammunition, not to mention a bulky rucksack containing spare clothes, washing kit, food and everything else. Whilst I knew about the PIAT I was not trained in its use and had little practical knowledge of its capabilities, having fired it only once and that was a year before in a stone quarry in Italy, when I was dismayed by its violent kick and obvious lack of precision. It was also believed that when the bomb found its target and the powerful 'hollow charge' concentrated its energy in a drill-like penetration of armour-plate, a metal ring from the tail flew back with equal force and smote the operator.

I might well have paraphrased what Wellington said about his infantry and applied his words to the PIAT: 'I don't know what effect it will have on the enemy, but, by God, it terrifies me!'

I ought to add that some people found it effective; indeed Major Cain disabled a tank with one at Arnhem for which he got the VC.[9] But many years afterwards I found that my distrust of this unwieldy weapon may not have been misplaced: the military historian Max Hastings has since observed, 'British battalions were equipped [for anti-tank purposes only] with a spring-loaded projector named the PIAT, which threw a 2½ lb bomb 115 yards and demanded strong nerves from its aimer, who knew that if he lingered long enough to fire at his target with a chance of success, failure meant probable extinction. Even in short-range tests in England, the PIAT scored only 57 per cent hits and was . . . cumbersome to carry, to cock and to fire.'[10]

We were called one morning to a briefing. This must have been Sunday, 17 September, at a time when the 'first lift' was already on its way from other bases. We were to be the 'second lift'. As usual both RAF and glider pilot aircrews shared the briefing which took place in the station cinema.[11] There was a large map on the stage showing the LZs and the flight-paths to them. There was not the slightest concession to security. The briefing was not detailed. Indeed, the wing commander commented on the lack of information, calling the whole affair 'rather a lash-up' but assuring us that all would go well. I remember no special military briefing. We spent the rest of the day looking to the stowage of the glider and meeting our 'load'. Mine was a 75mm gun-howitzer and a jeep loaded with ammunition, with a sergeant and some gunners. These were from the 1st Light Regiment, Royal Artillery, though nobody told me at the time.[12]

A massed glider take-off had now been honed to a fine art. The gliders were lined up herring-bone fashion along both sides of the runway with the tugs in the middle. I should say that in some pictures I have seen the position of the two components is shown as the reverse of this, but my memory is of the glider being on the edge of the runway. From the tail of the tug, the tow-rope snaked back in an S-bend across the tarmac to the wings of the glider.

We were due to start early on the Monday morning but the take-off was delayed by reports of fog over the LZs.[13] However, at last the time came for us to be bussed out to the glider to install ourselves and our passengers in it and to be dragged into the air. This part of the procedure did not go without incident. The previous afternoon on inspecting the load we had smelled something burning (an unwished-for aroma in a plywood aircraft with ammunition and petrol aboard). After about a quarter of an hour we traced the fault to some part of the jeep's electrical system which was being short-circuited by the pull of the straps holding the vehicle down.

Now, this morning, with the take-off actually in progress, I noticed that the compressed-air system was showing practically no pressure at all. This was serious. It would mean that on our final descent we would be unable to lower the huge landing flaps which were essential to putting the aircraft into a steep glide, checking the forward speed and thus making a spot-on landing possible. It would have meant descending in a long low glide, a good target for anyone below, with little control over where we finished up. Compressed air was also needed for manoeuvring with the wheel brakes on the ground during the landing run. There was no question of declaring the glider unserviceable at that late stage and opting out. Luckily, there was an airman around who had a compressor and with remarkable skill and coolness he got it connected up and pumping. He stayed at his task until the very last moment; indeed he only jumped out when the tow-rope was beginning to straighten and thus narrowly escaped accompanying us on our one-way trip. He had given us double the permitted maximum and, though there was a steady leakage throughout the flight, there was enough pressure left at the end for everything to work as normal.

We took off into a bright hazy afternoon on a heading which if continued would have taken us straight to France, but the flight plan provided for a long left-hand turn which took us northwards into East Anglia. Because of the nature of the load the glider felt unusually heavy and solid on the controls, but once we had dropped down through the turbulence set up by the Halifax tug-plane's four mighty engines, the flight was nothing out of the ordinary. Near the town of March we turned again, this time directly east.[14] We were joined by other aerial convoys and my recollection is of a long procession of tug/glider combinations spaced out along a single route, some slightly above and some slightly below us. Our altitude was, I think, some 7,000ft, with an airspeed of 160mph.[15]

The day had become sunny as we had flown northwards, and now we could see nothing but water below us, flecked here and there with slivers of white. These were the wakes of the air-sea rescue boats, reassuring in a way, but I remember speculating on how much chance there would be if one had to ditch with a gun and a jeep aboard. We carried no rescue equipment ourselves. The flight was a long one by glider standards, recorded as 2 hours 40 minutes in my log-book, but surprisingly soon the low Dutch coast came into view. Our course took us south of and parallel to the Scheldt estuary, and some of the islands were just shapes under water, flooded by the Germans. I did not know, could not have known at that time, that across this estuary the enemy had succeeded in moving a whole army which our ground forces had failed to cut off and which played a major part in the build-up of opposition against the 'airborne carpet'.

Flying straight and level over enemy-held territory in broad daylight gave one an odd feeling compounded of nervousness and curiosity, and your eyes were constantly searching for gun-flashes from the ground or hostile fighter planes in the air. As we approached our destination, we saw none of the latter and only a few of the former, but they were a long way away from the oddly detached world of our cockpit. Soon, however, dirty grey puffs of smoke began appearing, some at a distance, some close to and near enough for the sharp crack of the shell-burst to be clearly heard through the roar of the slipstream. We were not hit by flak, but in free flight I heard something zip through the wooden skin of the glider and found a bullet, still hot, on the floor. Somebody had been firing directly at us with a rifle or machine gun.

It had not been difficult to identify the landing zone (LZ). Rivers were always the best feature to fix one's position, followed in usefulness by railway lines. Our LZ was between the Lower Rhine and a railway, and the shape of the woodland at Wolfheze was exactly as shown on the air photographs.[16] I pulled off and, in contrast to my dive on D-Day, managed to put the glider down gently on its wheels in flat heathland, with hundreds of other pilots doing the same thing at the same time. Some gliders ran into others but there was plenty of room.

The records say that the second lift landed at 3pm.[17] It was a mild afternoon with the sun clouding over. Although we, the pilots, had completed the first part of our assignment, there were plenty of hours left in the day for other things to happen. We soon had the jeep and the gun out of the glider. Gathering our weapons and belongings we joined the gunners on the jeep and drove away across the sandy ground with the gun in tow. There were shots going off in the woods to the north and a few bullets whizzed over the heath, but there was no other sign that battles, as I now know, had been and were even now being fought nearby. We passed some crashed gliders at the end of the LZ. In particular there was one, a huge Hamilcar, lying completely on its back. It must have come in too fast and at too steep an angle, dug its wheels into the soft earth and flipped over. Its load would have been a heavy gun or a tank. What deaths its pilots had met, in their cockpit perched right above the cargo compartment, does not bear thinking about.[18]

The reader may well wonder what it felt like to be deep in Nazi-occupied Europe with the main body of the Army over 60 miles away, and separated from us by two major waterways as well as several small ones. For now that we were safely down on the ground the nervousness had disappeared, and all that was left, so far as I was concerned, was a sense of curiosity about what would happen next. We were, after all, part of a very powerful army, made up of a spearhead of paratroops who were reckoned to be the finest fighting soldiers in the world, together with airborne infantry, gunners, engineers, signallers and every other branch of the British Army, whose common denominator was that, collectively and individually, they had been selected and trained for just this sort of attack. We had not been told what opposition we might expect; either this had been unknown to our immediate commanders at that time, or if they had known, it had been found prudent not to pass the information on to us. According to Brian Urquhart, who was the Intelligence Officer to the British Airborne Corps, the presence of two re-fitting German armoured divisions in the Arnhem area was indeed known at Corps level, but his report had been brushed aside. In fact we had been told very little at all.[19]

That the land forces would arrive on time or thereabouts we had no doubt. Had the Allied forces not swept through Northern France and Belgium, brushing aside the broken remnants of the Wehrmacht? Did not the RAF command the skies, as our safe aerial convoy had amply proved? Had not the infinitely more risky operation of D-Day been an overwhelming success? These were the assumptions at the back of all our minds, even if they were not actually at the front. So all we had to do was to follow the rest of the troops into Arnhem and do what was needed to cope with anything we might find there.

Notwithstanding these background thoughts I recall no expectation that we would find it a picnic. It was obviously a dangerous situation to be in, and some of my comrades, even before we left the LZ, were looking distinctly glum. So we drove off along tracks and then along a road with various stops and starts and, as we noticed then, hesitations. There was no great sign of war until we passed a shot-up German staff car with a dead officer half fallen out: this was General Major Kussin, Field Commandant of Arnhem, whose body forms the subject of one of the few photographs that came out of the battle.[20] We had expected to proceed directly towards the town, our assignment having been to help form a screen round the north of it, but some miles short we were diverted off the road up a track to the left where the guns – we were with others now – were put in a field and we were deployed around.

Jim and I were first assigned a location in the front garden of a house on a corner where two roads met. We felt rather foolish cowering behind someone's front hedge on an apparently peaceful Monday afternoon. There were some civilians standing about, conversing together in low tones and taking no notice of us but constantly glancing apprehensively down the road we were facing. We saw no flowers, kisses, bottles of wine or cheers such as had greeted the liberators of other cities.

We did not stay in that position long. We were soon relocated with others on to an unmetalled road next to the field where the guns were and bade to dig ourselves in, which we promptly did. Very soon after we had dug our pit it became apparent, at this early stage, that things were not going well. No one told us directly, but there was some talk of a tank, and indeed ominous jingling sounds were coming up from the road where the civilians had been looking. Much worse, I overheard some officers in the field talking about whether they should now 'spike' the guns, i.e. damage or remove vital parts to make them useless to the enemy if captured. This was a shock: after all we had only just arrived and the guns we had brought over with no little trouble and effort had not yet fired a single shot.

Then something else happened. A couple of planes started flying over. RAF fighter cover had become the *sine-qua-non* of any operation, especially airborne ones, and we thought this was it. On the contrary, after making a pass or two, the planes came in low in a purposeful dive and started firing at us. They were not Hurricanes but Messerschmitts. On their second dive people began shooting at them with Sten-guns and rifles (there were no anti-aircraft guns with us) and one could see the shots hitting the armoured undersides, with total lack of effect. Overhearing another remark, I gathered that troops lining a hedge opposite had got the worst of it and that six of our people had been killed. This was not at all what we had expected.

I do not know how long we stayed on, or rather in, the road in a state of uncertainty – probably it was not more than an hour. All of a sudden, as is the Army's way, the gunners coupled the guns up to the jeeps, we sprang aboard and were making a fast exit along the road we had come down. At the main road we turned left and shortly after right into an area of housing which was, as we were to learn, the riverside suburb of Oosterbeek, some miles from the centre of Arnhem. It was Monday night, 18 September 1944. We stayed hereabouts until the final drama on the following Monday, 25 September.

We were in a leafy garden area, neither town nor country, a fringe of modern villas set among small fields and patches of woodland bordering on an older built-up area. A narrow road, metalled with stone setts, ran south towards the river, with, on one side, a row of new little detached houses. On the other side was a field of cultivated soil. Behind the houses was an area of allotment gardens with a fence and hedge on the far side.

It was already dusk when we arrived, and we were told to dig in against a hedge which bordered the far side of the cultivated field. It was quite comfortable here. We were inconspicuous from both the ground and the air and had a 'field of fire' in front of us. The day had been a long one, there was no obvious immediate danger, and, knowing nothing of what was going on elsewhere, we looked forward to some not ill-earned rest.

It was not to be. No sooner had we settled down than we were summoned out again and told to dig yet another trench, this time in the same field but at the roadside in the shadow of the houses. Personal considerations apart, I did not like this very much. If the Germans came it would most likely be from the direction of the far side of the row of houses from which they would be able to look down into our new excavations. However, like the other crews we dug valiantly away and soon that corner of the field was dotted with slit trenches.

The exact sequence of events during the next six days is not clear to my memory. I must thus abandon my attempt to write a chronological narrative in favour of a series of episodes which may not be in the right order. I can, however, distinguish three phases which overlap and merge into one another, and these will help to give shape to my story. On the first night we were part of a group of between ten and fifteen glider pilots from our flight under a captain and a lieutenant. After digging in we resorted to one of the houses on the road whose occupants had left. No formal guard was set but we took it in turns to watch from the back windows in the direction of the enemy. All was quiet, however, in our vicinity though there were sounds of shots going off further away. We spent the next day, Tuesday, in the same manner, and when we were not on guard we just sat around in the living room. It says something for our innate sense of propriety, or for our dreadful innocence of the realities of war, that the captain told us to tidy up the room – after all, we were in someone else's house! General Urquhart had noted the British soldier's respect for the property and houses of the people over whose land he fights. In ordinary circumstances such civility would be a creditable thing. Now he saw it as a time-waster.

At that time water was still available in the taps and lavatory and we used both. Later it ceased and the lavatory pan had to be filled with earth. Part of one night, and it may have been the first, we spent in the house's cellar. With the sounds of bombs and shots at no great distance I surmised what would happen if Jerry threw one of his grenades through the cellar window. I had a hip-flask of whisky with me then, a swig from which helped me and others to get some rest. But I felt safer in a trench.

During the first day there was an atmosphere of expectancy, which no doubt explains why we did little save keep a watch and sit about. We had not been assigned any role and certainly there was no sense of being under a higher command or of orders coming down from the top. In any case there was no obvious top. We thought that our situation was only temporary and that something would turn up. What should have turned up, of course, was XXX Corps, under General Horrocks, a powerful force comprising the Guards Armoured Division and two infantry divisions.[21] The operation having started on the Sunday, the link-up with ourselves should have happened on the Tuesday at best, certainly by the Thursday at the very latest. This is what we spent the time waiting for, and the fact that we were waiting, with every confidence to begin with, probably explains much of what was done, and not done, during the next seven days.

On the first or second morning the mortaring started. This became a regular feature of the first part of the week, starting at 0900 hours and going on for an hour, though later there were sessions in the afternoon too. When the bombs came over we took to the trenches, and Jim and I improved ours by burrowing under the road which gave us a solid cover on that side.

The mortaring was spasmodic at first but soon became intense. A mortar throws a bomb not unlike that which I have described for the PIAT. It is dropped into a tube and by its own weight detonates the cartridge in the tail. As it is projected high into the air, so it drops almost vertically – just the weapon against troops dug in. The first bombs came in twos and threes, some falling harmlessly in fields and gardens, others setting fire to buildings. I watched a splendid school go up in flames. First the thatched roof caught, then the interior blazed, finally a dull boom indicated that the water tank had exploded or fallen to the ground. Soon, however, the bombs came in clusters. The Germans had brought up multiple mortars a few streets away, and the bombs from these had a ghastly high-pitched scream, so you were well aware they were coming but would have no idea where they were going to drop.

One morning there was a particularly intense bombardment with bomb bursts all over the field. As Jim and I cowered as low as we could get, suddenly there was an ear-shattering explosion and the trench was so full of dust that I could not see my companion only an arm's length away. A bomb had burst on the parapet; three inches nearer and it would have been in the trench. We dug the tail-fin out later; it was buried deep, the force of the explosion having been absorbed by the dry sandy soil.

Looking out after one of these episodes I had the uncanny experience of seeing an apparently empty field. I thought all my comrades had been killed. In fact no one had been hurt and everyone still had his head well down. Had the Germans followed up with an infantry attack, the usual tactic, they would have found us literally sitting ducks. However, although there were no physical casualties, that is not to say that people were undamaged. It must have been as early as the Wednesday that some of the men began to cave in, and this seemed to begin with those who had represented themselves as being particularly tough or brash. They lost the will to make the least effort and could do no more than lie apathetically in the bottom of a trench. Men have limited supplies of moral courage in the same way that they have only just so much physical strength, and it is impossible to gauge this in advance. Those things which maintain morale – leadership, clear orders, a sense of common purpose – were not much in evidence. No one did anything to rally the faint-hearted.

I have since wondered what we did for food and drink, and, having no recollection of this at this distance of time, include here an extract from a newspaper item which I contributed to the *Herts Express*, the Hitchin local paper, in October 1944:

> The food situation was difficult throughout. Our 14-hour ration packs lasted double the time intended. Then we eked out the small supplies of food that reached us with vegetables from the gardens and bottled fruit from the larders. Most houses had a good supply of the latter. We had sufficient water until cut off from the pump we were

using ... In the last few days I existed on a cupful of stew and some biscuits.

In spite of the food shortage, I do not remember being bothered by hunger. I suppose we had other things to think about. It had been part of the plan that we should be resupplied by air, but the sky had remained overcast and neither friendly fighter plane nor transport had been seen. One day, the drone of many engines was heard, and out of the cloud appeared a flotilla of low-flying planes. They were mostly Dakotas, with a few Stirlings among them. (The Dakota or Douglas DC3 was the work-horse of this war, a steady twin-engined transport, easy to fly, and with a short take-off and landing run. The Stirlings were great four-engined planes originally intended as bombers but, having been found unable to attain the necessary altitude, had been converted to load carrying and other duties.) Flying at little more than 1,000 feet, steadily and slowly, these planes maintained an even course, and as they crossed the river, an inferno of anti-aircraft fire broke loose. They were so low that one could see the impact as a plane was hit. In some, a red glow started in the wing root (the Dakotas did not have self-sealing tanks) and quickly spread along. But not a single plane that remained undamaged fell out of line.

Some planes, streaming fire and losing height, just carried on and crashed beyond our sight. Others passed so close overhead that one could see the dispatchers at the doorway pushing out loads until the very last minute before flying away to their deaths. In one case two figures appeared clutched together with a single parachute. When it developed one of the men lost hold and fell like a rag doll, arms and legs all over the place. I am glad I did not see him hit the ground. A Stirling came in very low and almost seemed to stop in the air with a jolt. The gigantic machine slowly turned on its back, two parachutes appeared, and the plane dived into the ground just beyond my sight.[22]

I do not think I need comment on the sheer cold courage of these air-men who, knowing they were doomed, still did what they had come to do and dropped supplies even in the face of certain death. One was awarded the VC, posthumously unfortunately. It is perhaps the best tribute to them that, when they came over, the ground battle ceased. As if by mutual consent the mortaring and shelling stopped, everyone climbed out of the trenches and stood awestruck in the open. I have no doubt that the Germans, for their part, did the same. This air-drop and others later were some of the most tragic events of the whole battle – tragic because of loss of life, but tragic too because owing to communications failure, a now notorious feature of Arnhem, the drops were ordered for areas which were never in our hands. Some pilots saw our yellow recognition scarves and unloaded above us, but most did not. Nearly everything fell into the hands of the enemy. Among the containers which our people did manage to recover was one containing a complete kit of building tools and materials and one containing red airborne berets. An eyewitness to this later recalled:

> On my 28th birthday, 20 Sept 1944, I was taken prisoner at Arnhem. I remember seeing, early in the battle, a plane on fire above the dropping zone after completing its mission of dropping supplies. Among those supplies were new red berets to be worn at a victory parade which was to pass through the liberated town.[23]

It is historically a fact that these resupply operations were carried out without fighter support from the Tactical Air Force. In fact, during the whole battle of Arnhem the TAF was conspicuous by its absence from the skies over us. I understood that no air support was given until the Sunday (24 September), a week after the operation started. I have never read an explanation of this.

To begin with, the battle, so far as we were concerned, was a matter of waiting and watching – and at this stage hoping – until XXX Corps appeared on the opposite bank of the Rhine. We maintained some sort of vigil and retired to the slit trenches when the bombardment made it desirable to seek the security of Mother Earth. But all this was very inter-mittent: there were long periods when nothing was happening and we sat around in the sun doing nothing in particular. On one occasion I went to look for spades to assist in digging trenches. Finding a locked tool shed I blew off the padlock with my revolver, needing three attempts before it fired.

Once whilst I was keeping watch at a kitchen window, I thought I saw a movement in a house opposite and took the opportunity of letting off a few rounds from my Sten-gun. Whether it did any good – or harm – I never knew, but it helped to keep one's spirits up. As I was doing this a door which I had taken to be that of a cupboard suddenly opened and an elderly man emerged from a cellar. He said nothing to me but made sure the fire was stoked up. There was a family down below in this house, including a baby. We could hear it crying.

I heard later that a glider pilot watching from the same window had been shot through the head, his body being left where it fell till the end of the war. I do not recall how I obtained this information, but it is a fact that after the battle the whole of Oosterbeek was cleared of people and the houses devastated by the Germans, and that, as a result of their deliberate policy of withholding supplies, many died of starvation in the following winter. Operation Market Garden was an unmitigated disaster for the Dutch as well as for ourselves.

In the middle of the week, I was given a sort of roving commission to move about the area with the PIAT and be ready to engage any suitable target that came my way. In the open one was always at risk from sharpshooters invisibly sited in the houses opposite us, so I would dash from cover to cover with Jim and three bombs in a carrier plodding along in my footsteps. On one occasion I strayed beyond the allotments into the area of a neighbouring unit where I was encouraged to go out and look for a tank said to be around the next corner. It was not there, although a shot-up one, hit I think by Major Cain, was quietly smoking away up the street.

There were bodies on the pavement of the road beyond the allotments, lying where they had been shot down. They were glider pilots from our squadron who had been sent out on patrol for some reason or other. One of them was a regular soldier whose pride and joy had been an old-style pointed moustache which he used carefully to wax and tend. It was curiously sad that his little vanity had come to this. It may have been on the same occasion that we went into one of the older houses a little further up the road, a comfortable Victorian-looking place. There was said to be a self-propelled gun nearby and from an upstairs window I could just get a glimpse of it under some trees. I decided I could not get a shot at it and we left. Just as we emerged from the side door a couple of shells from the gun virtually blew the house up and in no time at all it became a roaring inferno. Two pilots who had been in a back room emerged, so concussed that they could hardly speak.

At this stage in my story it will help my future readers to understand our situation better if I introduce some words of general explanation. I also want to add some observations on how I, a lowly participant, saw the conduct of the battle. If these passages represent an amalgam of reading, memory and hindsight, they do not detract from my principal intention of giving an account of things as I personally experienced them.

Of the vast airborne army of over 10,000 men, which had landed on three successive days in several areas west of the city, only about 500, under Lieutenant Colonel Frost, reached the objective, the bridge. The rest, among whom was my small unit, were halted by the Germans, as we have seen, at least 3 miles short of it. We were then cooped up in Oosterbeek, having covered only half of the distance between the LZs and the bridge. The perimeter, as it came to be called, was an area in the shape of a sack. Its open mouth was to the south and bounded by the river, whilst its upper closed end was to the north straddling the main Arnhem-Utrecht road. The distance from north to south was about a mile and a quarter, while its greatest width was no more than about three-quarters of a mile, narrowing towards the river to about half a mile.

Within this area were some thousands of troops of all kinds. Many of them had had to fight their way into the perimeter from the north-west, as Geoffrey Powell graphically describes in *Men at Arnhem*. Others, having been repulsed with great loss in their attempt to get to the bridge along the river line, had grouped in the south-east corner near the church, where we were. As has been seen, the rest of us were in the sack from the first.

The impression has been given in some accounts, and particularly in the film *Theirs was the Glory*, that the perimeter was under unremitting attack and that the only thing that stopped it being wiped out was the gallant defence put up by those inside it. I have no intention of minimising in any degree the heroism and endurance shown by many individuals and units in many places at various times, but from my standpoint this popular view is not accurate. The men who reached the bridge were involved in some very fierce fighting, both in getting to the objective and in holding out there for four days. Almost to a man, everyone there was killed or wounded. Similarly, other units were heavily engaged both in attempting to break through to the bridge and in defending the landing and dropping zones to the west of the city.

However, in the case of us who were inside the perimeter the enemy were obviously content just to bottle us up and let time and exhaustion do the rest, while they attended to the much more serious threat down the road at Nijmegen and beyond. General Urquhart's account puts this more specifically and professionally:

The pressure on the perimeter continued, but it was spasmodic and tended to be staggered between areas, and none of the attacks was made at much more than company strength supported by a few tanks and self-propelled guns. Whilst it was possible that the Germans were contenting themselves with our gradual liquidation under the hail of mortars and shells, I was surprised that at no time was an overall, co-ordinated attack ever attempted. At this point the battle bore an odd character of suspense which caused me to ponder the possibilities that the Germans had other ideas in their heads. The probing and pestering at a number of points was understandable if the Germans believed that their colleagues beyond the river had the slightest chance of stopping the main advance of 2nd Army.[24]

Albert Seaton, writing from the viewpoint of the enemy, revealed that the latter's attention was concerned more with the effects of the operation on 15 German Army (the one between Arnhem and the sea), and with the attempted destruction of the whole airborne and part of the relieving force by a double pincer movement in the flanks from east and west, in the area of Uden and Veghel (i.e. far to the south of both Arnhem and Nijmegen).

There is another respect in which most of the published accounts vary from what I saw of the battle. They give the impression that the defence of the perimeter was conducted as an organised whole, improvised from whatever fragments of units remained after the casualties and confusion of the landings and subsequent actions, but organised never-the-less. This is probably inevitable, because most accounts were written by those who were trained, or preferred, to think in those terms. If it was so organised, I never became aware of it. Even allowing for the fact that the common soldier never knows what is really going on and what may seem a muddle to him may be a perfectly well-directed action when seen from above, he knows, sometimes all too well, whether he is under command or not, and apart from our own two officers who were in the same situation as ourselves, we neither saw nor were aware of anyone in authority.

According to Lewis Golden, the troops in the south-east corner, where we were, were first of all formed into a composite force called Thompson Force, later Lonsdale Force, after the names of the officers in charge, and later were part of the defence of the eastern half of the perimeter under Brigadier Hackett and then Lieutenant Colonel Murray of the Glider Pilot Regiment, when Hackett was wounded.[25] General Urquhart mentions visits to our area by himself and other senior officers, but of the command structure and of the visits, I and my comrades were totally unaware.[26] In fact one of my clearest memories is a negative one: how little our actions were under anyone's command or co-ordinated with those of other formations. It was a do-it-yourself battle (though the expression had not been coined then) so far as we were concerned. Only at the very end were some blundering attempts made to introduce some element of system into what we were doing, as I shall relate.

This absence, at the very juncture where it was needed most, of the normal hierarchy of command may be shown by the number of things which, in retrospect, ought to have been done but in fact were not. This I find one of the most surprising memories I retain from the whole affair.

We were not purposefully employed. There had always been the assumption that glider pilots on the ground had it as their first priority that they aided and abetted, and defended if need be, their load, until directed to do something else. Certainly the guns, or some of them, were across the field but we were not doing anything in relation to them, or as far as one could see, to anything else.

The trenches were not systematically dug. We were not assigned a particular position to man or a specific duty to carry out, such as holding this house or commanding that road. Indeed, my roving commission with the PIAT was a misuse of a weapon which, in a siege situation such as we were now in, should have been assigned a position and kept there at continual readiness.

There was also an absence of what might be described as normal army, and specifically infantry, routine. Guards were not set, and 'stand-to' and 'stand-down' periods were never ordered. No one had particular duties, no parties were detailed for foraging for food, water or ammunition. So far as I knew, no one assessed our state of readiness or had any vestige of a parade to see who was fit for duty and who was not. The whole established custom and practice of military life, which had been so irksome at home, failed at the very moment when it was most needed. In this I attach no blame to our officers: they were left as much in the lurch as the rest of us. This absence of grip, this failure of organisation, may have been part of the reason why some amongst us caved in early, as we all did to a greater or lesser degree in the end. The only reason, I think, why I kept going, a matter which was apparently the subject of remark among my comrades, as I heard later, was that I had something, however ineffective, to do.[27]

I cannot think that our experience was typical. It may simply have been that my small group had found itself in a backwater so far as the defence of the perimeter was concerned. It was certainly in a re-entrant angle, although there were no troops out front between us and the Germans, whom we could sometimes see walking about up the road. It may also explain why I cannot recall any member of our group being wounded or killed. In fact I saw very few dead bodies. The popular notion that the 'Heroes of Arnhem' spent their time manning barricades is far from the truth so far as I and my comrades were concerned. Apart from slit trenches dotted about absolutely at random, there were no barricades to man.

As to the performance of ourselves, the glider pilots, as a specially trained formation, most accounts speak highly of how we coped in various parts of the battlefield. I have no doubt that many rose to the occasion and turned their hand to whatever task presented itself to them, and this is borne out by many accounts I have read. However, without trying to detract from the validity of the overall concept, I think my experience shows a gap in its actual achievement. There was no doubt that our primary role was to be expert pilots of gliders, sufficient to get our loads and ourselves safely to the right place. In this I think we were highly successful. I think I can claim that we showed not only the skills required by flying (and it was said that only one volunteer in a hundred actually made the grade) but also a good deal of nerve and determination in making our one-way trips.

However, we had a secondary role, which was to be soldiers on the ground. It is here that the concept did not quite work out. Compared with our flying training, which was superb, our military training was surprisingly sparse. Individual things most of us could do, but we had no cohesion as a fighting unit. The flight to which we belonged and which found itself assembled in the row of houses in Oosterbeek had never operated as a section of infantry in training and did not do so now.

To emphasise this point I am inserting here an extract from Geoffrey Powell's *Men at Arnhem*, a slightly fictionalised but obviously accurate account of what the author experienced as a Regular Army major in charge of a company of paratroopers. His view of us is interesting and perceptive:

> I was a little worried by the glider pilots when I walked across to see them in their houses. They were intelligent young men, individualists, skilled in their esoteric art, but they were pilots first and infantry soldiers afterwards. As I talked to the staff sergeant in charge, the rest started to gather around in ones and twos, interested in what

we had to say but clearly disagreeing with some of it. They seemed disposed to discuss orders, perhaps because the orders came from a complete stranger, butting in on the conversation with their staff sergeant ... This easy-going approach was understandable, but in the circumstances it was hard to sympathise with it. The only way for us all to survive was for everyone to do what they were told and to do it quickly. The trouble was that these pilots were strangers. Their loyalties were to one another, and there was no reason why they should have any confidence either in me or in the men of the battalion. They accepted their orders with an ill grace.[28]

I pass over the subconscious attitude revealed in 'the only way for us all to survive was for everyone to do what they were told'. Colonel Powell candidly admits that many who did what they were told did not survive – for that very reason. But he is absolutely right in his main contention: we were indeed individuals, we had to be and were trained to be, in order to carry out our primary task in the air. On the ground we were expected to adapt to any role, and most did. That, however, did not give us the capacity suddenly to change and transform ourselves into an effective body of infantry or of anything else.

To resume my narrative ... The days and nights wore on and we lost count of the days of the week. To begin with there was no news of the forces supposed to be coming to our relief, and then news did come, but it was over-optimistic and not borne out by events.

For example, we were told on one occasion that the main army was well on its way and that we would be relieved on the morrow. On another it was said we would actually be seeing or hearing the Army on the opposite bank at 1100 hours. This was not just soldiers' talk but factual statements put about. Although they may well have originated in such scanty information as was coming through about what was happening down south at the Nijmegen bridge, I believed then and believe now that they were officially circulated in a crass attempt to keep our morale up. Of course it did just the opposite.

I continued scurrying about, to no good purpose. One day, arriving breathless in a room of camouflage-smocked figures, I heard references to 'the prisoner'. Looking around I perceived amongst our people a man very similarly dressed, who told me in German, 'the German comrades went away and the British comrades came'. I think this was a result of one of the small infiltration attempts which happened occasionally. The man was a stone-mason from Munich. He had been brought up the Rhine from anti-aircraft duties at Rotterdam and disembarked at Arnhem only the week before. I assured him he would be well treated. I do not know what happened to him.

Another odd incident occurred one morning when nothing much was happening and we were sitting around outside one of the houses. Two men, civilians, strolled up the road and one, in good English, started to talk to us. He compared my PIAT to the much better German equivalent. After a little while they walked off.

This did not seem in the least strange at the time. There were a few civilians about, some apparently members of the Resistance who later came over the river. The only thing that crossed my mind about the visitors was why two able-bodied civilian men were wandering about in the middle of a battlefield. If they were some sort of spy, as I thought later, their openness and casualness had been their protection.

One afternoon, returning to my base, I was met by some of my flight who told me in matter-of-fact terms that we were no longer in our usual house. Apparently, they had been sitting around when there came a knock on the door. On opening it they found a German soldier. For a long moment each eyed the other, the German disappeared round the corner and our man shut the door. Believing, I suppose, that the enemy was getting too near for comfort, they did not contest the issue but just moved to another house down the road.

It may have been this house or another, for we were in several at different times, where in a quiet interval I rifled the owner's desk. It was No. 70 Benedendorpsweg, and I know this because I brought away the owner's membership card of the Dutch National Socialist Sympathisers Association. I also purloined, as spoils of war, some stamps which I added to my brother's collection.[29]

The loss of this base created difficulties for me, for when I enquired what had happened to my rucksack and Jim's I was told that they had been left behind. I had nothing now but what I stood up in or held in my hands. Presumably some German was now picking over my spare clothes, appropriating my best airborne beret with its solid silver badge, drinking the rest of my whisky and enjoying my remaining food and cigarettes. He would also have found my fighting knife, a bloodthirsty-looking dagger I had preferred not to have about me in the circumstances we were now in.

Also abandoned were my Sten and its ammunition and the spare pack of bombs for the PIAT. I never learned why and under what exact circumstances my colleagues had yielded the house. This may have been a further instance of failing morale. It never occurred to me to go back to investigate.

There now supervened a stage which I can only designate as corporate languor. I have read since that one of the effects of a long period of bombardment (and we were bombed every day and shelled as well) is the creation of apathy. Lack of food and sleep and a gathering feeling of stalemate when no progress was visible added to it. Yet I recall no trace of defeatism. Everyone I think still had confidence that things would turn out well and that we should be relieved. All we had to do was just hang on.

Most of the men now either lay in their slit trenches or on the floors of houses. Some of the infantry who had not succeeded in getting to the bridge had come into our area; they were so exhausted that they were incapable of doing anything else. A few managed to keep active, one in particular who went about with a Bren gun until he was shot in the leg, and others trying to salvage containers from later air drops which had become lodged in trees or on roofs. Soon it became impossible to collect these, or do anything else in the open by daylight, without certain risk from snipers whose locations were invisible to us.

The mortaring, shelling and small-arms fire continued with shorter intervals between each barrage. There were sounds too of flame-throwers in use against the position on our right, a series of ugly screeches. It now became the practice of the enemy to send a tank or armoured vehicle down the road beyond the allotments every morning and afternoon to engage the occupants of some buildings on that side. Its custom was to fire a few shots which were replied to, and then go away. The skirmishes were short and noisy, the tank being opposed by fire from Bren guns and a captured Schmeisser machine gun, the rapid fire from which was unmistakeable.

As I have said, we were in an angle of the perimeter and the tank attacks were not followed up. Strange as it now seems, its visits became so regular and familiar that after the first few we took them for granted, even though it was only a hundred yards away. The unspoken thought seemed to be that, if it was anyone's business, it was that of the people opposite. At one stage I suggested to an officer that one of the guns should be brought up to engage it, or alternatively that we should fell a tree across the road (using explosives if we could find any) but was told, 'we have other plans'.

116

One night there were sounds of activity from the place where the tank usually positioned itself, and I, still prowling about, thought I would get near to investigate. My impression was that the tank or whatever it was had either broken down or had had a track damaged. I could hear the Germans talking about 20 to 30 yards away and especially an educated voice saying '*Hier ist ein leeres Haus*' (Here's an empty house). What they were doing there I did not discover. I think they had brought up another vehicle to tow the damaged one away. There was a nasty smell of ersatz diesel fuel.

I was minded to worm my way forward with the PIAT to see if I could get a shot in, which would have involved quietly creeping through the bushes and making a hole in the fence, but my faithful Jim insisted on coming too. In vain I asked him to leave me, because this was a job for one, and then ordered him, as I had no confidence in his fieldcraft. He still refused, and at last I had to take him back to where the other men were and start out all over again.

This time too I found myself not alone. An officer had come up, evidently with the same idea as myself. He tiptoed towards the hedge and lobbed over a phosphorous grenade in the general direction of the tank. This momentarily lit up the scene, was answered by a few shots, but achieved nothing except the loss of surprise. I gave up. Having been thus foiled, I thought I would nevertheless still fire the PIAT and send a bomb vertically into a nearby street where I judged the enemy might be. I spared my shoulder the shock of the recoil by putting the butt against a tree. There was no sense in this and I did not hear the bomb explode.

My story now comes to the last stage. From about the Thursday on, when, as of course we only learned later, the party on the bridge were finally overcome, the bombardment became more intense and the lulls between the storms shorter and more infrequent. There was more artillery shelling and more of the hideous noise of flame-throwers, and the area was several times strafed by fighters. There was not much option but to keep one's head down. We had now left the houses on the road and were in one of the buildings at the base of the rectangle formed by the allotments. It was a single-storey dwelling, possibly a holiday bungalow. People were standing and lying about in the rooms and it was here I heard the first and only expression of defeatism when someone said to me 'I don't know why they don't just come in and wipe us all out.' At the back there was something like a lean-to greenhouse. I asked who was in it and was told that a sergeant was dying there. This explained the blood on the hallway floor. I looked at the sergeant who was unconscious, lying on a table. He had been bandaged up but no one was with him. This sounds both casual and callous but there was no medical post in reach that we knew of, the ambulance jeeps with stretchers on the roof had long ceased running about, and to try to carry him away would have been suicidal.

One night – of the Sunday as it happened, though we did not know that – the Captain told Jim and me to stand down and try to get some rest, so we found a slit trench at the back of the house. The Germans were not very active at night, and we soon dropped off into the usual half-waking doze, only to be rudely woken some time in the small hours by an angry command. We found a strange officer glaring down at us in the moonlight, waving a pistol and demanding our names and unit. He accused us of the serious crime of sleeping whilst on sentry duty: for this we could be court-martialled and shot. He refused my protest that we had been ordered to stand down. Then he wandered away but that was the end of sleep for that night. It was also the end of such vestiges of morale as I had managed to keep up.[30]

I have no idea who the officer was, to what unit he belonged, or whether he similarly threatened other men. It is only since I have been writing this memoir that the thought has occurred to me that he might have been out of his mind.

It was now D+8, Monday, 25 September. We did not know it of course but this was the morning beyond which General Urquhart considered we could no longer hold out. (His message to General Browning drafted on the Sunday night is given in the Epilogue.) Early in the morning we were again in the slit trenches facing the allotments when another strange officer appeared. He was a young and small lieutenant, from I know not what unit, but he was certainly not one of ours. The main thing that struck me about him was that he looked remarkably clean, well-fed and rested, quite unlike us haggard specimens. Without explaining who he was or what he was doing, he ordered me to take up a position well forward of all the rest, half-way up the path in the middle of the allotments, and there keep watch for tanks.

I was not very keen on this. To stand about outside was to court death, and the position indicated was completely without cover and in full view of anyone or anything who or which might be in the houses which overlooked the allotments or coming down the road ahead of us. In any case there was only one bomb left, for out of the three remaining I had discharged one and the tail of another had somehow got bent. Also, however one was supposed to engage a tank with a PIAT, I did not think the best angle was from in front in direct view of its guns and where the armour was thickest.

This I told the officer and proposed as an alternative that I should take up a cut-off position at right angles to the path from which I could attack any intruder from the side. I also asked him to organise supporting fire from the men to our rear around the house. This he agreed to do. So I moved with Jim perhaps 20 yards to the left. We were now backing on to the houses we had vacated days before which were supposed to be in the enemy's hands, and I was uncomfortably aware of their upper windows and those of the other houses at the end of the allotment balefully staring down at us. It was only a matter of time before someone took a pot-shot at us; indeed it was surprising that no one had done so already.

We stayed there a short while, looking around for some sort of cover, but there was none. I thought of the possibility of trying to dig a trench but doubted if the enemy would give us time for this even if we could summon up the energy. There was no sign of activity among my comrades, no weapons were at readiness, and the officer had disappeared. There seemed no good reason for staying where we were. We returned to the trenches with everyone else.

The day resumed its normal pattern. As the morning wore on it became sunny, and all was as usual. Even the sound of the tank coming down the road on the other side of the allotments was as usual. Something, a change of sound perhaps, made me lift my head out of the trench. A most horrible sight met my eyes. The tank had not gone down the road but had turned into the allotments and was lumbering straight at us. A tank looks gigantic from about 20 yards away.

It is quite extraordinary to recollect, and evidence of the situation then prevailing, that not one out of all of us there had been alert enough to see the tank turn off the road, no one had fired at it, no one had given any warning. All I did was to shout 'Look out, tank!' and run for it. I ran obliquely, with someone else running beside me. The tank was firing its machine gun, my companion gasped and was perhaps hit. I tumbled into a gun pit, wrenching my knee. I remember thinking, idiotically, that this was not fair, we had done our best so far, they ought now to give us a break. After a moment or two to get my breath, I jumped out and put the house between myself and the tank. To my astonishment Jim, weaponless, appeared round the other corner.

I never learned precisely what the tank did. One returned prisoner-of-war of our squadron later told me that it had positioned itself across the slit trenches where it had systematically shot up the guns in their positions nearby. As it fired, its tracks had sunk deeper and deeper into the soft turned-up earth and my informant had had his legs trapped under them. Most of the men around the house presumably surrendered, but how and to whom (for I saw no infantry following up), I never enquired. It was too painful an episode to talk about, and no one ever did. Geoffrey Powell, however, says,

> It was fortunate that the scale of the German attacks lessened a little during Monday. For all that, the gun positions were penetrated during the morning, clearly in an attempt to cut the British off from the river, but the Germans were pushed back with the help of the remaining 75mm pieces, manhandled to fire over open sights at ranges down to 50 yards.[31]

Jim and I were now on our own so far as any military formation was concerned. We went towards a large building which I think was the church, and if the reader wonders why I am unclear about so obvious a point, it is that we were not exactly sight-seeing and in any case, only went down into the basement from the porch. There were some people there not doing anything in particular and not under anyone's command. One of them was a major who gave it as his opinion that 'we must be bloody aggressive'. He could get on with being aggressive without us, I considered. So we left the church and began hunting along the lower river bank with some vague idea of finding a boat but there were only some wrecks in a boathouse.

We prowled westwards, being not by any means the only ones who were also drifting about. At one stage a group of soldiers, seeing my rank, seemed disposed to attach themselves to me, but I had nowhere to lead them to. We came to a mansion where someone, perhaps Mrs ter Horst, one of the Dutch heroines of Arnhem, thrust a mug of some sort of stew into my hands. I really did not want to eat it, but did so nonetheless.[32]

By this time the area was under virtually continuous bombardment. The enemy were using a type of shell which exploded in the air low above us, sending pieces of metal whizzing through the trees. One man near us was hit; it is surprising that more were not. So far as I had any intention, and it was not a coherent one, it was simply to find some refuge from it all, a burrow where like an exhausted animal I could curl up and rest. There was no shelter around the house, so we wandered westwards into a more wooded area. In a hollow we came across a party from our own squadron, men known to us. They were silent and looked at us incuriously. There seemed no point in joining them and no one suggested it, so we moved on.

At this juncture an even heavier bombardment came over. We jumped into some slit trenches, Jim asking the occupant of one, 'Room for one more, chum?' The man, a Polish soldier, made no answer: he was dead. We talked to another Polish soldier hereabouts. He told us he had been in a parachute drop on the south side of the river. Some of his companions had landed in trees, where the Germans cut their throats as they hung from their harness. The only weapon issued to many of them, he said, was a Gammon bomb, a bag of plastic explosive with a detonator, which you had to throw at or drop on a tank – assuming you could get close enough.[33]

Sometime later we found ourselves at another house, a small mansion in its own wooded grounds, which must have been near the most westerly edge of the perimeter. Here was quite a large party of glider pilots from a different squadron under an officer. The same incurious atmosphere prevailed. We asked if we could join them, this was agreed to, and we were assigned to a trench on the edge of the garden overlooking a field. I believe someone gave us a few biscuits. There was nothing to do but wait. It must have been about six o'clock when someone came down from the house and told us that we were to be withdrawn across the river that night.

The reader may or may not have noticed that so far I have said nothing about fear. Of course we were afraid in a general sense all the time. But that was nothing unusual. Flying gliders day and night was a matter of fear; it was an ever-present companion whom one took for granted. I do not remember being abnormally afraid at any time during the previous part of the week, even when running in full view of the tank; perhaps a surge of adrenalin prevented me from being so. Much of the sensation had been that of curiosity.

Now, however, unalloyed, unremitting, merciless terror took possession of me. I literally shook from head to foot. My body was like a cold jelly, my jaw chattered. For about half-an-hour I was incapable of any thought, let alone action. I did not just experience fear; I was possessed by it. After a bit I gained control of myself, though from now on the terror did not leave me. I do not know why this happened at this time; it may have been the thought that the crossing of a wide river, with safety on the other side, was a hazard worse than any we had survived so far. Or it might have been the welling up of all the terror I had accumulated but had suppressed during the previous days.

As a first step to moving down to the river some of us were told to clear the drive which ran through the front garden. There were branches knocked off trees, but, in addition, the corpses of two horses which had been alive in the field in front of us when Jim and I took over the trench. The poor beasts had somehow escaped from their field and had been killed by the air-bursting shrapnel which had continued to come over. It had rained, and the horses were wet. We each took a hoof and dragged the bodies clear, blood gurgling out of a throat wound at one end, excreta from lax sphincters at the other. Then there was a wait. Well into the night we waited and finally the word came to move.

Stories have been told of boots muffled with strips of cloth, white tapes indicating paths, glider pilots stationed to act as guides, men holding on to the tails of each other's smocks. That may be the official account and doubtless was the case in other parts of the perimeter. For ourselves, we saw none of it. We had hardly left the road when the file of men stopped. We were aware we had joined a column of hundreds of hunched men winding endlessly away into the darkness.

It was raining hard now and the moon must have risen behind the thick cloud because we could see a short way ahead and around us. A Bofors gun was sending a tracer shell horizontally across the river at half-minute intervals to mark the direction of the withdrawal and the limit of the crossing area.[34] There was a continuous curtain of shells falling around the north of the horseshoe-shaped perimeter, laid down by the guns of XXX Corps from miles away.

We waited, edged on, waited again in the pouring rain. There was some mortaring and shouting away to our left, but nothing near us. We gradually got closer to a gap in a hedge which we thought was the river bank. Passing through this at length, we were dismayed to find we had still some way to go. It was the edge of a wide flood plain, and the plain was full of men. There were some signs of control visible when we first got near the water with small numbers of men being assembled into groups, but the dark was now beginning to turn grey and order was beginning to break down. We had been told we would be taken off in boats, and while we had not known what to expect, any expectations we had were dashed by what we now saw. The boats were little bigger, or so it seemed to our eyes, than seaside rowing boats, propelled by an outboard motor. (I have since read that they were 'assault boats' holding fourteen men). In the growing light we could see only two of them – so few for so large a number.

Jim and I had been near when one of the boats had come across from the other side. It was immediately rushed. I would not call the mood one of panic but rather of desperation. Men were throwing themselves towards and into the boat, some grasping the gunwale and bidding fair to capsize it, some missing and plunging into the deep water and going under, weighed down by their heavy boots and helmets, not to be seen again.

To me rescue looked impossible. Some men were stripping off and swimming. I considered doing this but there was a fast current and the opposite bank, which we could now see, looked too far away and the river between all too visible. Jim was in any case a poor swimmer and I did not feel I could leave him on his own. The river bank was not a regular line but one with frequent groynes forming small bays. I had decided it was hopeless to try to get across and we were actually walking away with the intention of holing-up in a house until we either escaped or were captured, when a boat with another in tow came in to one of the bays right in front of us. We both ran to it, I stepped into the towed boat and from that into the other which was a little further out. I did not see Jim again till after the war.

Following us there was a rush of men who literally tumbled into the two boats (this as I learned later knocked Jim over the far side into the water). The helmsman, a Canadian engineer sergeant, tried to stem the rush by firing his automatic rifle towards them, but nothing could hold back the desperate men. The boat I was in was crammed, the other almost over-whelmed, completely full, with people in the water grabbing at the sides with others inside trying to hammer or lever off their hands.

The boats swung out into the stream. The light was fast coming up and one felt the surge of terror as we wallowed on the water, exposed to any enemy machine gun both up and down river. The two craft were so heavy that they could not be steered and began drifting with the current. The helmsman gave the order to cut the tow-line, which was taken up by others. I, seemingly the only one with a knife, did so, leaving the occu-pants of the other boat trying to paddle with their hands and rifle butts. I do not know what happened to them. There were some men in the water holding on to our boat which now gathered way. There was one just below me almost being dragged under, so I lowered my hand and grasped the collar of his smock until we got across. When the boat grounded all the men vanished in an instant; all my man said was 'Water's damned cold' and left.

I too got out of the boat. For a moment or two I lay on the bank revolving the ideas of going back to help the solitary helmsman and to find my co-pilot. Unfortunately, the animal instinct for self-preservation got the upper hand. It was now fully light. I doubt if anyone else got across. Ours was probably the last boat.

I climbed over the steep embankment and found a young soldier of the Dorsets dug in on the other side. I said I was glad to see someone in a proper helmet, his being the traditional 'tin hat' compared with our air-borne rimless variety. He looked mystified at this silly remark coming from a staff sergeant and silently offered me a cigarette.

There was no reception party on the other side, only people on a road all going in the same direction, so I followed them. Some had swum over completely naked and had been given articles of clothing by Dutch women from nearby cottages. I found or was handed a pair of women's shoes which I substituted for my boots, which, while soaked through, were still perfectly good. On these I tottered into a farmyard which was evidently an assembly point. A newspaper correspondent looked at me curiously and I realised what a ridiculous figure I was cutting. I put my boots back on. I cannot account for this aberrant behaviour.

As we stood about in odd groups being given mugs of tea, an officer evidently became aware of how exposed everything now looked across the river, and I heard him say 'By God, they need smoke.' The artillery barrage had continued all night, putting down a curtain of exploding shells round the north of the perimeter, partly I believe to deceive the enemy about the intention to withdraw and partly to cover it. Soon curling streamers of smoke began to streak the lower sky, settling a white mist all over the ground, where it stayed on this damp windless morning. Through this pall the houses and trees of Oosterbeek could be dimly seen, a fitting winding-sheet. It was a scene of Lot and his family fleeing from the burning Sodom and Gomorrah in a Victorian engraving. I could not but think of those still over there, so close but beyond aid.

A truck came along and took us the 10 miles to Nijmegen. There on the wayside were the DUKWs, big amphibious vehicles, half lorry, half boat, which should have ferried men across the river. Because of the steep bank it had proved impossible to get them down to the water – a surprise to someone, no doubt.

At Nijmegen we were taken to a building which only a week before had housed German soldiers. There was an illustrated magazine there with pictures of the Katyn graves. On the wall was chalked *Parole: Heimat* ('The watch word is homeland'). By borrowing someone's razor I scraped five days' growth of beard off my face, and we must have been given something to eat, not much, but what it was I have forgotten. One room was set out with double-decker bunks, and here we were supposed to rest. I hung up my belt with its ineffectual revolver on the bedpost and when I was out of the room for a moment someone stole it. I did not regret the loss but it seemed odd in our then circumstances that anyone should have thought of doing such a mean thing. A bearded sergeant said hello to me. I did not recognise him until he told me he was the gunner sergeant I had carried over. It seemed a lifetime ago.

Among my comrades who had survived I found my friend Peter, the same who had also solo-ed under Tex Parker at Abbots Bromley. For a moment I became quite emotional on finding him alive. As we dozed off into an uneasy sleep, a sudden crashing woke us again. Nijmegen was being bombed. I could not tolerate the idea of being cooped up in a building no doubt well known to the enemy as quarters for troops, so Peter and I set off through the streets, with evening now coming on, until we found a school, where in a classroom we slept under a table throughout the night. Even then there were flashes and explosions outside.

The next day there was some talk of a parade in the presence of General Browning, the Commander of the British Airborne Forces, and that everyone was expected to have a weapon in his hand. It is indeed recorded that the dapper, exquisitely turned out Browning did address the remnants of his troops, but if I attended he made no impression on me for I have no recollection of it.

We were then taken on a further truck journey down the much-fought-over road, but I have little memory of the debris of war which must have littered it. What I do remember is that we again came under fire. Mortar bombs burst around, the convoy stopped, and, looking out, I saw a soldier dragging a half-severed foot around the back of a lorry. Again I had the feeling that this was very unfair. We ended up at Louvain, a subdued party. Of our flight which had started out with forty-seven officers and men, the survivors autographed Dutch banknotes as souvenirs. I still have mine with the signatures – all eight of them.

On Thursday, 28 September we were quickly transferred to Brussels airport and were flown to Ramsbury in Wiltshire. Before the day was out we were back at Brize Norton. It was now, if anywhere, that the full impact of what had happened really struck home. Whether spontaneously or by accident we returned to the self-same billet we had so cheerfully left exactly three weeks before. There were the thirty or so beds, each one still holding the aura of its previous occupant. We instinctively gravitated to our own. Opposite and on each side the beds were empty. Our mates had gone. The flight, the squadron, the 1st Battalion even, which had been the matrix in which we had had the whole of our military being, had to all intents and purposes ceased to exist. No one said very much, but the faces of our RAF comrades in the sergeants' mess showed that we were not the only ones that had been hurt. Then there was a de-briefing when we were asked particularly of glider pilots we knew to be dead. Then we were sent home on leave.

Sending us home on leave was probably the worst thing that could have been done to us. In the light of later knowledge our homecoming should have been handled in a very different way. We were not only exhausted by a gruelling physical experience but had gone through one which would correctly be called traumatic, i.e. one which had done damage to the personality. It would now be identified as 'acute stress reaction' character-ised by 'persistent re-living of traumatic events through dreams or flash-backs, withdrawal from others, impaired memory and survival guilt'[35] and some form of therapy would have been applied. Nothing was done.

I have experienced some but not all of these symptoms at varying times, but, strangely for one who has always had vivid dreams, I rarely dreamed about Arnhem after the first few months. But the memory of the events there have formed a sort of back-drop to the rest of my life, with my day-to-day living played out in front of it. In the Army we rarely talked about them, and until now, forty-four years after, I have never been able to tell the whole story to anyone.

Chapter 12

After Arnhem

Nothing was ever the same after Arnhem. I was a good deal disgusted with my own un-heroic performance, and no man likes to learn the truth about himself. Many are fortunate enough never to have to do so. But I was more than disgusted with the Army. As previous parts of this memoir have shown, I had slight confidence in the Army's expertise or application to its task, but that it could gamble one of its best formations in an impossible and fruitless escapade was at least credible. That it could fail to adapt itself to a situation which ran counter to its pre-arranged plan and find itself unable to snatch even some slight advantage from it, showed, in the light of what I had seen, a degree of ineptitude not wholly unexpected. But that it could allow the lives of so many of its fittest and most highly trained men, airmen as well as soldiers, to be frittered away to no purpose at all and in such a casual fashion was beyond belief.

Perhaps I lacked, and still lack, some element of understanding of what war is all about and of the way it is conducted, but, whilst the exquisitely planned and successfully executed D-Day operation had raised my respect, or perhaps more accurately mitigated my dislike, I now felt that the Army had forfeited any claim to call on one's trust and confidence ever again. But there was nothing to be done about it. The Army retained its grip and could do with one what it liked. After leave, B Squadron assembled at Earls Colne aerodrome near Colchester in Essex.

Nationally there was a bleak feeling after Arnhem. The fifth winter had set in and after the summer's optimism it was now clear that the war was still not won. The enemy seemed to have infinite resources, if not of materials, then of capacity to organise what he had left. The impression grew that he would never give up and would have to be fought to the end. There was talk of an 'Austrian redoubt' where it was expected Hitler would withdraw to and there meet a *Gotterdammerung*-like end.

It was a very subdued group of glider pilots which gathered at Earls Colne. What I have said about the effects of Arnhem upon me must have been the experience of many. Gone was the panache, the buoyancy of spirit, the small incidents of fun-making which had given flavour to our lives. Naturally I missed very keenly the company of my congenial mate Jim Donaldson, whom I felt I had left in the lurch and whose fate was of course at that time unknown. I was not particularly friendly with anyone else. There were no nights of gaiety in the mess, and I cannot recall even a visit to a pub.

I did not fly again until 10 November when we resumed cross-country flying in Tiger Moths and later in Horsas. The Tiger Moth flying for me was marked, or marred, by two incidents, neither to my credit. On one routine cross-country I was accompanied by a young second pilot hitherto unknown to me. We flew up into East Anglia on a pleasant sunny afternoon and, all going well, I became overconfident and careless with my map-reading. The technique was to fly from 'fix' to 'fix', i.e. from one positively identified point to another, working on a quarter-inch map, meanwhile noting and correcting any divergence from the required track. Cloud began to come in from the sea. I did not worry at first because I knew we would soon cross a railway line from which I could fix my position. The cloud thickened and came lower. Asking my co-pilot to do the flying whilst I concentrated on the navigation, I found that, whilst he could fly straight and level well enough if he could see the horizon, he did not know how to fly without it. He had had no training in instrument flying, neither had he any idea how to read a map. In the conditions we were now in he was of rather less than any help.

With one hand on the stick, the other holding the map, and trying to look at it and the ground whilst flying on the instruments, I simply could not fathom where we were. The cloud-base came down lower and lower and I had to do likewise, until we were flying well below the regulation 1,000ft. Presently we did indeed come to a railway line but it was running east and west and not north and south as it should have done. But at least I had a ground feature (though I did not know which railway it was) and I determined to stick with it. I proceeded to fly up and down, trying to get a fix of some sort. We kept coming to a big chimney poking up through the murk, but not being able to see much around it, I failed to pinpoint it on the map.

I was beginning to wonder whether I ought to try to find an open area of some kind to put down in, which would almost certainly have ended in a crash, when all of a sudden I spotted a small railway siding branching off the main line. It was marked on the map. The town with the chimney had been Halstead which I had flown around before but now had failed to recognise in the mist. It was only about 3 miles from the aerodrome.

Visibility was getting worse and worse and I had to fly lower and lower in order to keep the ground in sight. Almost at treetop height I found Earls Colne railway station, but even from there the aerodrome was not visible. Luckily, I knew the lane which connected the village to the airfield and I followed that along from above at no more than about 100 ft. When I got there the control tower was flashing the green permission to land through the now thickening ground fog, and I went straight in. As we taxied across the grass the engine began to cough. Another few minutes and we would have been out of petrol.

The other incident did not have a happy ending; indeed its consequences were of some seriousness to me and another. I was setting out one day from inside the hangar when an aircraftsman prematurely and incautiously started to swing the propeller. There was a drill for this. We were supposed to follow the routine of calling out 'switches off', replied to with 'switches off'; 'suck in' – 'suck in'; 'contact' – 'contact'. Having uttered the last response, the erk would give the prop a mighty swing and jump clear as the engine burst into life. Familiarity bred contempt: the routine did not always get followed.

As captain I was responsible for what happened. In the Tiger Moth the 'off' position of the switches was downwards, the reverse of most electrical switches, and as I reached over to check them (they were outside the fuselage), I evidently for a brief moment had them in the 'on' position. During that moment the erk, who should have waited for my order, began to swing. Unfortunately, the engine fired (only once; thank Heaven it did not continue firing) and hit the erk's hand, doing some damage. There was an enquiry, I was charged, and the blame was equally shared. The erk was adjudged to have received punishment enough, and mine was a severe reprimand. This should have been endorsed in my log-book but it never was. I believe Major Toler, our officer commanding, was kind enough to forget to have it put in. It was a blot on my record, nevertheless.

There was another episode around this time when I made some bad landings and began to think that my eyesight was becoming faulty. The MO assured me that there was nothing wrong with my sight. One does not have to be a psychologist to see that my subconscious was telling me I wanted to get out. Just before Christmas, which I suppose I spent at home, I was sent down to Tarrant Rushton in Dorset to be 'converted' onto Hamilcars.

The Hamilcar was an enormous cargo-carrying glider, like the others completely made of wood. It was said to have a wingspan greater than that of any other plane then flying. Unlike the cylindrical Horsa, this one was basically a square box sitting low on the ground with a blunt lift-up nose and a long raised rear fuselage. The entrance was through a side door into the spacious hold, a room about 15ft high. There was a ladder up the wall via which one climbed out on to the plane's upper surface and across the vast wing. Here was a tiny cockpit about as big as a Hotspur's, with a Perspex canopy under which the two pilots sat, one behind the other. From this position the thing which one most needed to see to be able to judge the landing – the ground – was about 20ft below. As one flew, the wings flexed up and down in a most disconcerting fashion.

The Hamilcar's flying characteristics were quite unlike those of the other two gliders. They were slow and ponderous machines, taking a long run to get off the ground. In the air they were steady, too steady, responding slowly to the controls. The landing angle was flat, so that one had to pull off a long way from the objective and approach in a shallow glide, sinking rather than diving. Over enemy territory they made easy targets, and I remembered the one I had seen at Arnhem. The Hamilcar course was intensive. My log-book shows five circuits on some days and two long cross-country flights. I did not like the Hamilcar, though I was successful in flying it. By now my heart was not in flying anyway. About the middle of January I was back at Earls Colne again, thankful that I had not been allocated to Hamilcars permanently.

Whilst I had been away something had happened to the regiment. At Arnhem we had lost about 75 per cent of our strength, with many killed or wounded or, as was happily proved later, still alive though prisoners of war (in fact I have read somewhere that we sustained more casualties proportionate to our numbers than any other unit in that battle). Then Chattie, not one to allow himself to be overcome by such a minor setback as losing most of his command, had an idea. He realised that the Air Training Schemes which were in full swing in Canada were producing more pilots than would ever be wanted at this stage of the war. He asked for, and got, a large number drafted in. The fact that they were RAF and not Army was supposed to make no difference. When he announced this to us, which he did personally to each squadron, he laid stress on the fact that the RAF types were fine upstanding examples of all that was best in the junior service and that they had been specially picked to join us in our less prestigious task. Whether he really believed this I do not know, but with due respect to him he was wrong on both counts. The ones we got, qualified pilots though they were, were mostly lacking in that illusive quality of 'presence', and many had grievances, the biggest and perhaps the most justified of which was that they had been compulsorily transferred to us.

The RAF intake were mustered into flights, and I was put in charge of one of these. Obviously, these fellows were bitterly disappointed that they were not to have the glamour of flying Typhoons or Mustangs, and they showed their dislike of being with, and under, us. In contrast to our good-humoured tolerance of the Army's peculiar ways, they lacked every vestige of the sort of *esprit-de-corps* which we had developed, did not hesitate to enlarge upon every inconvenience, and were prone to question, even from the ranks of the morning parade, the most routine orders. There was not much to be done with them. They had had a modicum of both glider flying and battle training before they joined us. Whether it was deliberate policy or not, Army and RAF never flew together.

That winter was extremely cold and uncomfortable. I recall the trees around our billet – we were in a country estate – festooned in hoar frost like the palace of the 'Snow Queen'. Naturally I got home as often as possible. Waiting for the train on the outward journey or for the station transport on return, we could watch from the elevated platforms at Kelvedon station the flying bombs stuttering their way to London, often pursued by a fighter. Once or twice, I heard the V2 rockets. Their roar through the air followed the explosion by a measurable period of time.[1]

Chapter 13

Operation Varsity

In February and March 1945 the Supreme Allied Commander, General Eisenhower, implemented his plan for a three-phased advance into the Rhineland. In the south, General Patton was to advance his US forces through the Palatinate and then achieve a number of Rhine crossings around Mainz and Coblenz, before advancing towards the River Elbe and a meeting with Soviet troops advancing westwards.

Meanwhile Field Marshal Bernard Montgomery's 21st Army Group would advance on the northern flank. Under Montgomery's command, the First Canadian Army would cross the Rhine and swing north towards the coast above Amsterdam.[1] At the same time he would direct the Second British Army to deliver the main punch along a twenty-five mile front and cross the Rhine at Wesel, just above Düsseldorf. Montgomery also had under his temporary command the Ninth US Army, which he would direct to cross the river and encircle the vast industrial Ruhr area.

To enable the Second British Army to gain a foothold on the eastern bank of the Rhine, an airborne assault, called Operation Varsity, would follow several hours after the river crossings. This vast air armada would amount to the largest airborne operation ever carried out in one location on a single day. The assault would involve the 6th British Airborne Division and the 17th US Airborne Division, the latter having fought as infantry during the recent Battle of the Bulge and now due to undertake its first airborne operation.[2]

The 6th British Airborne Division had recently been retraining in Britain and was now entrusted with securing targets on the east bank of the Rhine, just north of Wessel. The division, comprising the 3rd and 5th Parachute Brigades together with the 6th Airlanding Brigade, was to capture Diersfordter Forest, including the high vantage point of Schneppenberg. These forces would then move on to secure the village of Hamminkeln and the three bridges that spanned the adjacent River Issel. Once these objectives were taken, the survivors from the 6th Airborne Division would then link

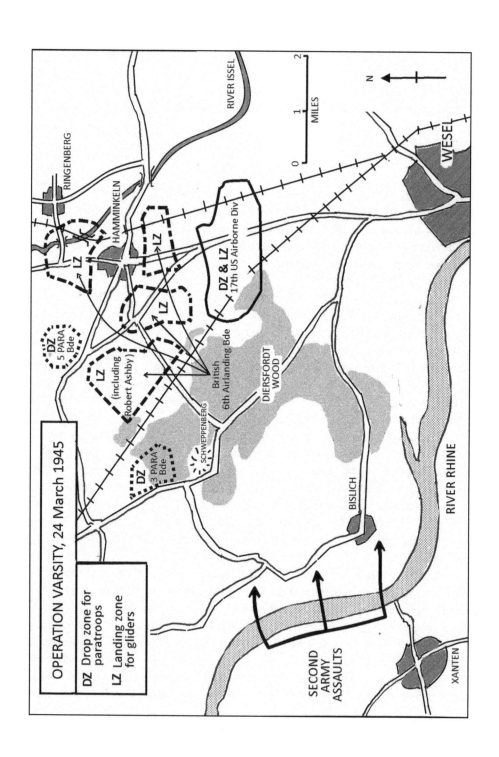

OPERATION VARSITY, 24 March 1945

DZ Drop zone for paratroops
LZ Landing zone for gliders

RINGENBERG
RIVER ISSEL
HAMMINKELN
WESEL
N
MILES
0   1   2

DZ & LZ
17th US Airborne Div

DZ
5 PARA Bde

LZ

LZ

LZ

British
6th Airlanding Bde

LZ
(including
Robert Ashby)

DIERSFORDT
WOOD

SCHWEPPENBERG

DZ
3 PARA Bde

BISLICH

RIVER RHINE

SECOND
ARMY
ASSAULTS

XANTEN

up with the Second British Army for the push up towards Kiel and Wismar on the Baltic Coast.

The Glider Pilot Regiment, now heavily reinforced by RAF pilots after its losses at Arnhem, was attached to the 6th Airborne and allocated to eleven airfields across East Anglia, including Earls Colne in Essex.[3] *On 24 March 1945 fifty-five tugs towing Horsas took off from this airfield and one of these gliders was piloted by Robert Ashby. He was in a Horsa Mark II, containing a jeep, radio trailer and crew, setting off to join up with the massive air armada heading out of East Anglia. The British parachute brigades were transported by Dakota aircraft, while the gliders carried the 6th Airlanding Brigade, together with support vehicles, light artillery and vehicles. The British aircraft made a rendezvous over Hawkinge in Kent and then set course for Brussels to join up with aircraft bearing the US 17th Airborne Division, which had set off from French airfields, mainly in Curtis Commando C-46 transports. Beyond them lay a 100-mile flight and finally the silver streak of the Rhine.*[4]

The 6th Airborne faced a depleted enemy, whose ranks had been shattered in continuous fighting back towards the Rhine. Nonetheless, those battalions which had survived were expected to put up ferocious resistance especially as they were now defending their homeland. Allied intelligence had identified that enemy forces included units from two parachute divisions, two infantry divisions, 15 Panzer Grenadier Division and 116 Panzer Division.[5]

The planning for Operation Varsity was haunted by the legacy of Arnhem, but some important lessons had been learnt. For this time the airborne troops, both parachutists and glider-borne, would not be dropped and landed on the east bank of the Rhine until several hours after Allied land forces had crossed the river. Furthermore, the airborne troops would be dropped, together with air-landing forces, in one lift and their supplies would be delivered by transport aircraft shortly after the landings.

The assault was preceded on 23 March 1945 by a massive air and artillery bombardment, designed not only to degrade the German defences on the other bank, but also to prevent Field Marshal Model's twenty-one divisions being brought forward to reinforce the enemy positions. To this end, railway centres in the Ruhr were heavily bombed, bridges and viaducts destroyed, and Luftwaffe airfields were put out of action. German communication centres, such as Münster, were attacked, while enemy headquarters, barracks and camps were strafed and rocketed by RAF Spitfires and Typhoons. Just before zero hour, the adjacent town of Wesel was virtually flattened by repeated bombing waves by Lancasters and Mosquitos.

However, the operation did not quite go according to plan. Although it was carried out in daylight on 24 March to achieve better cohesion of scattered paratroops, it left the air armada highly visible to enemy anti-aircraft units. Furthermore, the gliders, containing men of the 6th Airlanding Brigade, were towed into the Rhine airspace early, before the Allied fighter-bombers had completed their attacks on the enemy anti-aircraft positions.[6] Consequently, the glider pilots had to contend with intense ack-ack fire, and also pilot visibility was severely reduced by the thick smoke and dust drifting across from the attacks on nearby Wesel. Fortunately, they did not have to contend with attacks by the Luftwaffe, since enemy fighters could not break through the air cordon created by Allied fighters during the early hours of the operation.

Despite the difficulties encountered, all objectives were achieved by 1400 hours on 24 March and Operation Varsity was a complete success. But it was not without cost. The British 6th Airborne Division lost 347 men killed and over 700 wounded, while the US 17th Airborne Division lost 359 killed and over 500 wounded, with nearly 650 missing in action. The enemy anti-aircraft guns had taken a terrible toll of aircraft and gliders. About fifty-five aircraft were also shot down on 24 March, including a number of C-46 paratrooper transports which ignited due to fuel leaks. The 6th Airborne lost ten gliders shot down, while 201 gliders crash landed and yet more were destroyed on the ground by enemy fire.[7]

Within days, Allied engineers had built twelve bridges over the River Rhine suitable for heavy armour, and the northern route into Germany was now assured.

*   *   *

At the beginning of March, purposeful exercises with cryptic names like 'Nosmo' and 'Riff-Raff 2' began, so we began to suspect that an operation was in the wind. We did some long flights. One weekend I was at home on leave when the phone rang recalling me to base immediately. This was a bad experience. It gave me and mine a sickening feeling for we knew what it portended: it meant that the next, and probably the last, operation was only days away, and whatever form it took it was bound to be pretty desperate. Having received the message, which required immediate compliance, I sat down and momentarily fell asleep. My mind refused to accept what was happening.

Back at Earls Colne there was now all the fuss and bother of preparing for an operation, and having charge of a section, I got a double share of it. There was my own load to meet and agree procedures with and their equipment to install in the glider. This time I had an RAF squadron leader, a former fighter pilot, with a jeep and trailer, the latter containing a radio set via which close-support Typhoons were to be directed on to ground targets.

Then there were things to be done for the men in the section, with weapons and ammunition to be collected and to see distributed, and all the other paraphernalia. People kept pressing more and more equipment on me: binoculars, a prismatic compass, grenades, until I was so heavy I could hardly walk. In the midst of this I was summoned to flight-test an officer's glider. It was so nose-heavy that I could hardly get it off the ground and had to superintend the rearrangement of the load.

Then there was the briefing, and had we not become pretty fatalistic by now and immune to surprise about anything, it would have evoked a few gasps of astonishment. The plan was simple in the extreme. It was for us to put down not near, behind or in front of the enemy, but right on top of him.

Since the failure the previous September to 'bounce the Rhine' (in Montgomery's schoolboys' phrase) at Arnhem, the Allies had gradually approached nearer to this wide and fast-flowing river barrier, delayed by winter, by flooding by the enemy of low-lying ground, and by the Germans' counterattack in the Ardennes around Christmas 1944. There was competition among the Allied commanders to be the first to stand on the eastern bank. For this the palm went to the American General Patton, whose men had found the bridge at Remagen undestroyed.

The main thrust, however, had to be made across the flat lands of Holland and north-west Germany. The northerly thrust having failed, the axis of the attack was now directed to the east. The first task before invading the North German plain and reaching Berlin was to get the weight of the Allied armies (for there were several of them, with the British now in the minority) across the river. The area chosen was in the neighbourhood of the town of Wesel, a short distance inside the German border and not very far upstream from Nijmegen and Arnhem.

The concept of the airborne part of the operation was entirely different from those that had gone before. We were to go in after the main assault, which was to begin on a wide front during the previous night in an amphibious crossing reminiscent of D-Day. It was expected that, when it had progressed 5 or 6 miles, the impetus of the attack would be slackening and coming up against a defence line which the Germans had fortified in and behind the Diersfordter Forest. We were to descend squarely on top of and within this defence line, swamp it, and so help on its way the invasion of the Reich. Surprise would be achieved by delivering an airborne army, in broad daylight, after the main army had moved, and not before, as had been the case with all previous airborne operations.

Our briefing consisted of little more than telling us it was going to be a long flight over the North Sea, Belgium and Holland, and that we were to land in small farmers' fields between the forest and the town of Hamminkeln. I recall no photographs, only maps showing our allocated field which we hoped to be able to locate by reference to the river and the forest. I remember a general but undefined sense that this was the last throw (for us at any rate) and that everything was just being piled in without too much finesse.

Take-off was early the next morning, and preparations went on well into the night. The padre held a communion service which was attended by many, who felt perhaps that if ever the comforts of religion were necessary it was now. It was then I realised why the Christian faith had had to be based on the idea of a prolonged and painful sacrificial death. Nothing else would have matched the possibilities now before us.

When at last everything was ready, I went out into the dark and into the countryside nearby. It was the park of some stately home and there were enormously thick ancient oak trees there. I sat down with my back to one of them and gave myself over to thought. I remember, even now, the train of my thinking. I was quite certain I would not see the next day out. It was not a premonition and there was nothing mystic about it. I just knew that on the morrow I would be dead. After surviving two operations it was impossible I should survive a third. And the nature of this third operation was such that survival was out of the question.

I reviewed the course of events which had brought me to this place and time. I had been born in the middle of one war, had been badly affected by its aftermath, and was now ending my life in this one. The whole thing had a symmetry and an inevitability which I was quite prepared to accept.

I had written a letter to my young wife which she rightly construed as a farewell. I knew then that later in the year she would have my child. It was enough.

I thought of the tree behind me. It had stood through centuries of events which made the present ones by no means exceptional. It had certainly seen men marching off to Passchendaele forty years before, and to Waterloo a hundred years earlier. Most probably it had witnessed the gathering of forces of roundhead against cavalier. It might have seen, as a sapling, the beacon fires signalling the approach of the Armada, or even the men mustering to go with Henry V to Agincourt. For them it had been the same as it was for me. One man's life was nothing in the perspective of time. I had lived, I had experienced, I had had some measure of happiness. Now, evidently and to some extent regretfully, it was time to go. Having thus mentally detached myself from all that had gone before, I walked back to the huts.[8]

There was only one thing special about this flight and that was that I experienced a frisson of fear as the English coast disappeared behind us, something I had not known on previous flights, but it was quickly suppressed. Forming up over Kent the British gliders formed three great lanes flying towards the Continent, and met the American air fleet over Wavre, just south of Brussels. Then we flew north-east following hundreds of paratroop planes. There were gliders all over the sky: 855 American Wacos and 440 Horsas and Hamilcars, the greatest air fleet of gliders of all time.

After we entered Holland the river came up very quickly, and indeed we were moving fast, being towed by a Halifax. I began searching the ground, looking towards where we expected to find our LZ. I handed over the flying to the co-pilot whilst some miles away to get a general view of the landing area and seeking to identify from the shape of woods, rivers and bridges where approximately our farm ought to be. However, when we got nearly there, nice judgement was out of the question. The whole area was covered with smoke. I believe most of this had been put down to cover the river crossing and had not dispersed, but it had been added to by burning buildings and the general fog of war. Great patches of ground including that where I had hoped to find our LZ were invisible.

Over the river dirty grey-black puffs suddenly started to appear in the air around us, much thicker than on previous operations. My co-pilot, whose first op. it was, asked me tremulously whether this was flak, but I assured him it was no more than smoke. For the run-in we followed the usual practice with my co-pilot doing the flying while I tried to locate the LZ from the map. I could not do so. The 'Tail-end Charlie' (rear-gunner) of the Halifax told me later he would always remember the look of bafflement on my face just before we pulled off.

Indeed I was baffled, but pull off I did in what I thought was approximately the right place, steadied the glider to its slowest speed and began a curving descent. In the two minutes or so of the glide I gave up hope of locating the farm I was supposed to be aiming for and simply searched for somewhere to land with the moments for choice rapidly ticking away. Quite near the ground I glimpsed, ranged along a hedge, a whole troop of soldiers with unfamiliarly-shaped helmets. That's done it, I thought, I am coming down amid a German Army patrol. Such was not the case. They were a stick of American paratroopers who, bless 'em, had landed in the wrong place (a not unusual happening among Yanks) and fortunately they were clearing the area.[9]

Ahead was a small field, scarcely more than a paddock. Full flap, a dive and levelling out, and we were rumbling across the grass. Unfortunately, there was a wide water-filled ditch at the far end, and in this our nose wheel ended up, with the glider undamaged and cocking its tail up in the air. We were about a quarter of a mile away from where we should have been – not bad, all things considered.

My squadron leader told me afterwards that in all his years of flying he had never experienced anything so exciting as those last few minutes between pull-off and landing. We had been lucky. Of the 416 Horsas and Hamilcars which reached the battlefield, only eighty-eight landed undamaged. Of the remainder all were hit, mostly by light flak and small arms fire, and thirty-seven were completely burned out.[10]

There was a good deal of shot whizzing about, and with one accord the squadron leader, I and my co-pilot dived into the ditch despite the water. From there we saw some nasty sights. We were by chance on the safe side of a farm building now in friendly hands, but the fields around were commanded by emplaced German 88mm guns. As the gliders came in they were shot up one by one. Some came down burning. I remember, in particular, an American Waco which, right in front of us, just disappeared in a flash of flame. Nothing seemed to be left of it. Others were hit whilst taxiing to a stop.

All this happened in no time at all and presumably the guns were overrun. We set about the task of getting the jeep and radio trailer out, but this was a Mark 2 Horsa and with its nose in the ditch we could not get at the front-loading door. We tried to pull her out of the ditch but she would not move, so we started to drop the tail off. However, with every volley of shots outside we kept most unheroically running back to the ditch. Presently we pulled ourselves together. My memory is hazy about what actually happened, but the difficulty I seem to remember was in pulling the securing wires out of the bolts which held the two parts of the fuselage together. We achieved it in the end and the squadron leader duly drove off.

The battle where we were lasted only about two hours, but of the three landings I had taken part in, this was by far the worst. The infantry soon came through. I thought it impertinent of them systematically to go into every glider looking for loot. Apparently, the specialised airborne axe was highly regarded. My co-pilot went off somewhere leaving his rucksack with all his belongings on the ground. He never saw it again.

If I had done what I ought, I should have now sought out my section, and, under the officer, an RAF flight lieutenant, taken charge. But I could hardly believe that my conviction had, so far, proved false and that I was still alive. I was not going off wandering in open country risking being shot by the enemy (and I did not know where he was either), or, more likely, by our own side. Finding some of our regiment under a captain in a farm nearby I put myself under his command. We asked a German woman for water which she provided, saying, 'yes, five o'clock, time for tea'. I reflected that had we been proper soldiers we would have been inside raping her.

I spent the night in a trench. Next morning, apart from a few stray shots coming over, the battle had moved away. The captain asked me to go with him to look at the wrecked gliders and see if we could identify any of the dead pilots. In previous operations the news about casualties had been very slow in coming through. The day before I had seen the bodies of a group of soldiers who had tried to run from their glider to the relative safety of a ditch nearby. They had been cut down by gunfire, their severed arms and legs looking like pieces of meat. The ditch was full of blood. I had also seen a parachute on the ground under some trees, and, it being a sort of domestic standing order that one should bring back useful lengths of otherwise unobtainable nylon, I thought I might as well collect it. But it had a peculiar smell. I then noticed the corpse of an American paratrooper hanging in the tree above. The parachute was soaked in his blood.[11]

This morning, however, I saw things even more grim. Most of the gliders near us were more or less completely burnt. In some cases the fire had consumed not only the whole fuselage but also the wings, which white ash and metal control cables now outlined on the ground. In some crashed machines thirty bodies remained strapped in their seats, or what was left of seats, or tumbled about outside. In others there was no more than a hummock of grey ash, stained here and there with red. We looked at several but after a time I felt I could take no more. I told the officer so: he understood.[12]

During the day I found out where my section was and we repaired to a farmhouse for the night. They settled themselves down in the farmer's beds but, remembering Nijmegen, I could not tolerate the idea of being confined in a building, so I slept outside in a trench. I only felt safe in the arms of Mother Earth.

I have little recollection of what happened then and none at all about how we got back to the UK. With the Squadron reassembled in Germany, the Padre conducted a short open-air service to which quite a number of us came. Getting home first, he was kind enough to phone my wife with news that I had survived. I also recall exploring a windmill, which had been used by the Germans as a sniper's post, with a young glider pilot who happened to live in the same road as myself in Watford. I think he had come over after the operation as part of a baggage party.

Some very subdued German civilians began creeping out of their houses, all old people, and reading the placards put up with remarkable speed by AMGOT (Allied Military Government of Occupied Territories), which obviously had everything ready for the occupation of the Reich. Every form of fraternisation was forbidden and I did not speak to them. I wondered how they felt with the curse of National Socialism lifted from them and have no doubt that many welcomed it.

We never got any news about casualties except what we circulated among ourselves; presumably this was official policy or maybe it was thought that it was not our business to know. In *By Air to Battle*, it is stated that 'casualties among the glider pilots amounted at the end of that day to between 20 and 30 per cent killed, wounded or missing'.[13] Another report says that seventy-seven British glider pilots were wounded and another 175 killed or missing.[14]

Of individual cases I heard only few particulars. One man, Doug Harrison, was shot as he fired a Bren gun at a fortified farm just after he had leapt from his glider. Captain Norton, who had been with us at Arnhem (and who had spent the previous night writing letters), was killed as his glider was shot down. In the nature of our task, if one were shot down or crashed on landing there were very few, if any, witnesses who could say how or where one had died.[15]

The RAF men who had formed the section I was supposed to be in charge of, came through intact: all credit to them. They were pleased with themselves, rightly, and there was a much better spirit among them afterwards. I even got quite friendly with some. Two of our people had an extraordinary escape. Their glider had had its tail blown off while still high up. The remains, totally out of control, plummeted downwards, but before hitting the ground the wreckage, by some freak of aerodynamics, began to spiral like a sycamore seed and landed the pilots safely. The first pilot told me he had found it impossible to believe he was still alive.

A feature of this operation which distinguished it from the others was the number of 'premature releases', i.e. cases where the glider parted from the tug before reaching the objective. Some of these may have been genuine malfunction of the towing gear, broken ropes, or trouble with the tug's engines, but in others there was some sort of human intervention. Nothing much was said but gossip had it that the pilots concerned were put under arrest, charged and faced with court-martial for desertion in the face of the enemy. I never heard if this actually took place, or what resulted if it did.

One incident in the Rhine crossing was seen by many, though not by me, and was often talked and written about. A Hamilcar was flying at normal height approaching the river when its load, a tank, suddenly burst out of the cargo hold and hurtled to the ground. The glider broke up; all aboard were killed. It was thought that the bottom of the glider gave way, the only known instance of a glider breaking up in the air. To my mind a better explanation is that the tank driver, given the order to start the engine, did so but forgot that he had put it in gear.

It seems to me peculiar, and also a pity, that the Rhine operation has not apparently attracted and held the attention gained by both D-Day and Arnhem. Certainly it lacked the glamour of the one and the pathos of the other. Operation Varsity, as it was called, was, I believe, the largest airborne operation ever mounted, and was the last in which gliders were used on a large scale. It thus has a place in the history of warfare. Apart from that, it was the most daring and drastic airborne assault ever conceived, and it was the one which required of its participants more resolution, and (if I may be allowed to say so) courage, than any of the others – and that is saying something. When it took place, the tide was rolling so strongly in favour of the Allies and against the Germans that it made only a slight difference to the tempo of events. Perhaps that is why it is not much remembered.

Chapter 14

The End of the War

There is not much more to tell. .... In July we were sent up to Shobden for a few days and there I had my last two flights, in a Mark II Hotspur, with one of the same instructors who had tutored me over two years before. In the meantime he had risen from flight sergeant to flight lieutenant. I have often been asked if I ever wanted to fly after the war, but no, I never had the least inclination to do so, quite apart from the lack of means and opportunity.

After the Rhine operation there was talk of the Regiment being sent out to India for use against the Japanese. Happily that never came about. There was also talk about some of us being offered commissions, but I went to the colonel and told him I did not want one. It would have meant committing myself to a further period of active service and that was just what I did not want. I got the impression that some in the Regiment wanted to ensure its continued existence into peace-time.

In the summer some of us were sent down to Devon to establish a sort of holiday camp at Watermouth Castle near Combe Martin. I was placed in charge without being given the rank, and, especially among the RAF, it was difficult to preserve even a small evidence of military discipline, and I could not bring any enthusiasm to the task. Our commanding officer made various attempt to keep the men usefully employed. Some helped on the land but others, grotesquely, were assigned to a laundry. Their stories were very risible about the ironing of women's clothes.

It was here we received the news of VE-Day (Victory in Europe) which the paternalistic government arranged in advance. I spent it totally alone, not having the stomach for the synthetic celebrations got up by civilians who had never been near the war. There was a newspaper headline: 'It's all over.' Not so, I remember thinking, it's just about to begin. And on the international, national and personal levels, I was right. It is only now in 1990 as I write this memoir that it is permissible to think that the Second World War is really over.

Towards the end of the year we were again at Hampstead Norris doing nothing in particular and it was possible to get home fairly often. It was from here that I obtained weekend leave to visit my first-born. Returning to camp from Reading station on a dank Sunday night, the crowded 3-ton lorry slid on wet leaves, the canopy hit overhanging trees, and jagged ends of metal tore through the standing men. Some were badly hurt, one with all his front teeth knocked out, others with skull and shoulder injuries. Most tragically, a young lieutenant who had just joined us was killed, some said by trampling feet. The wrecked canopy knocked my red beret off. Once again death had brushed my face and had passed me by.

The last scene of all was on an aerodrome at Tingewick, just west of Buckingham. It was not operational and we were left very much to ourselves. I spent some time trying, with a friend, to fit out a clapped-out Austin Seven which I had incautiously bought. It served us for a little while until I got rid of it on someone else.

The only military activity which some of us were called upon to carry out, happily not including me, was to mount a 24-hour guard of honour in a local chapel for the body of Admiral Lord Keyes, the famous veteran of the First World War Zeebrugge operation. I am sorry to say that my comrades whiled away the night hours by playing cards on his coffin.

The Army was making some small gestures towards refitting us for return to civilian life, and set up an education centre with a small library. I was placed in charge of this and spent many placid hours reading. I was released in March 1946 having served exactly six years. When demobilisation did come it was hardly more ceremonious than my call-up had been. An officer we had never seen before, and who was obviously just 'going through the motions', interviewed each man, asked us rather perfunctorily about our civilian prospects, and bade us farewell on behalf of the Army. Then it was understood that if we made our own way to the demob centre at Luton we would be fitted out with civilian clothes and discharged.

The civilian clothes were largely unwearable – I remember I had to send my suit back, so unwearable was it, with the comment that it might be suitable for an habitué of a billiards saloon. We were given a gratuity of, I believe, some £200 in the form of a credit in a Post Office savings book. With a sense that one era in one's life had closed and a new one opened, we all went our separate ways, not without some nostalgia for the better things of Army life, the comradeship, the mutual support and loyalty of men to one another, and the sense of all being in the same boat, whatever that boat consisted of. These things were not to be found outside.

But the Army did not set us quite free of its clutches even then. We were not, strictly speaking, demobilised. We were transferred to the 'Z-Reserve'. This meant that, at any time and without notice, it could claw us back and put us in the ranks again. This actually happened to my younger brother who had spent most of the war in the gruesome conditions of a Japanese prison camp. One would have thought that he had given enough. But the Army had no sentiment: its men are not men but commodities.

I have sometimes been asked if I received any recognition for my services. The answer is 'no'. Although I believe I am one of a very small number who took part in and survived three operations (although there are some living who took part in four) and am human enough to wish that a 'gong' of some kind had come my way, the only acknowledgement I ever received was a letter from our officer commanding, joining us all on to the Distinguished Flying Cross (DFC), which he was awarded. Nor was I, or anyone I knew, included in any of the victory or investiture parades of which there were a number at the end of hostilities.

There was a glider pilot contingent in the big Victory Parade in London but the talk was that it came from the nearest depot and included men who had never seen action of any kind. As a kind of ineffectual mute protest, I did not apply for such medals as I was entitled to, until, forty years later, I became curious to know what they might be. They were exactly the same as I would have received if I had remained a driver in the Royal Army Service Corps (RASC) and had served in the same theatres of war. However, when I think of the tour after tour of thirty operations which the bomber crews had to put in, or the steady attrition of the infantry put into attack after attack, I think that what I did was unusual rather than exceptional. And I enjoyed a lot of it, particularly the flying.

In due course I was back in the Hitchin Library. Some of the readers remembered me, but six years is a long time and most did not. One who did was a gushing woman. 'Hello, Mr Ashby,' she said. 'How nice to see you back. And did you have a wonderful time?' I was totally unable to reply.

My last paragraph is probably unfair to the generality of Hitchin people. Many years afterwards I was making conversation with a long-standing local resident, and to establish common ground I said I had been involved with the opening of the new Public Library and Museum in 1938. 'I don't remember anything about that,' she said. 'What I do remember are the extraordinary things you did in the war.' So far as I know, this lady and I had never met before.

Chapter 15

Epilogue and Reflections

The origins and formation of the Glider Pilot Regiment

With the publication in 1992 of *The History of the Glider Pilot Regiment* by Claude Smith, it has become possible to add a few more details to my memoir.[1]

The raising of a force of parachutists and glider-borne troops had been ordered by Winston Churchill as early as 21 June 1940, an act of both foresight and optimism in view of the fact that the last of the 'little ships' had left the Dunkirk beaches only on the 4th of the same month. Everything had to start more or less from scratch, including the design of troop-carrying gliders. The prototype Hotspur first flew on 5 November 1940, and the specifications for other gliders, one of which became the Horsa, were laid down at about the same time. The prototype of the Horsa first flew on 12 September 1941, and the initial order was required to be completed by July 1942. It was thus still a newly introduced aircraft at the time I joined the Regiment in that month, and there was much to be learned about its use and capabilities.

The Glider Pilot Regiment was formed with effect from 24 February 1942, a requirement being that its personnel should be drawn from volunteers already serving in the Army. During the previous eighteen months there had been a running argument between the Army and the RAF about which service ought to provide and control the new formation, with Sir Arthur Harris, later known as 'Bomber Harris' and chief of Bomber Command, throwing his weight on the side of the RAF. He is reported as having believed that glider flying and towing required no special skills and that existing RAF pilots could master them after a course or two, returning to more conventional duties until wanted for an airborne operation. It was even thought they could receive enough training during the period of run-up to an operation once it had been decided upon. Harris also voiced reservations about the competence of army people – 'even infantry corporals' – to fly. However, as we know, the Army viewpoint prevailed in the short term, though it seems the controversy did not die and that we might well have been absorbed into the RAF later on.

At first glider pilots were referred to as 'coxswains', thus bringing a naval term into an already confused situation (or is my memory correct that this was used for the helmsmen of airships in the First World War?). Someone pointed out, however, that the naval analogy was incorrect as the pilot's job, unlike that of the naval coxswain, would not be over when his craft touched land and disembarked his passengers. Finally, it became realised that glider flying was a specialised skill and that the pilots would have to be kept in practice by continuous flying of large gliders, so far as this could be provided.

Training in glider flying started during 1941, largely on an experimental basis, with twelve Army pupils and sixteen volunteer bomber pilots. Later, it seems, in line with Harris's view, a hundred RAF pilots were involved but 'had quickly become disenchanted', so that scheme had not been a success. It is interesting to note, however, that for the very first operation involving towed gliders (Operation Freshman), aimed at a heavy-water plant in Norway, the Army supplied one crew and the Royal Australian Air Force the other. All met their deaths, some in crashes and some at the hands of the Germans in a wartime atrocity for which those responsible paid the penalty later.

It was on 29 September 1941 that it was definitely agreed that the Army should provide the pilots and that the RAF should train them. The Army personnel were to come from the 5,000 volunteers who had applied for transfer to the RAF. Applications for such transfers had been first invited during 1940 but had been suspended during 1941 (when, as I was later to learn, the Army eventually got wise to the fact that it was losing some of its more intelligent and fittest people – not that the Army ever set much store by intelligence).

'Total Soldiers'

As I say in my account, I don't recall when I first heard of the Glider Pilot Regiment and had the opportunity to volunteer for it. The Regiment had been formed under an Army Order with effect from 24 February 1942 and my application and subsequent agitation must be placed between April and July 1942 when we were in the mill at Beyton, near Stowmarket, Suffolk.

I was therefore a fairly early member of the Regiment and one of the last entrants to the 1st Battalion. The 2nd Battalion was formed in August of that year.

The History of the Glider Pilot Regiment comments on the excessive strictness of Chatterton's regime, which was in contrast with the outlook of the first commanding officer, Colonel Rock. It suggests that many outstanding men were lost to the Regiment as a result of some minor infringement of turnout. Rock thought too much drill would result in a ham-fisted pilot. But Rock was killed in September 1942 on night-flying. Whatever the truth of the matter I never thought that the discipline at Tilshead had any negative effect on one's capacity to fly. In fact being able to survive it was a great morale-raiser after the mind and body-numbing experience of the turgid RASC.

Overseas

As my account shows my unit arrived in North Africa in July 1943 but too late to take any part in the Sicily operation. We joined the people already there just as they were returning from Sicily and several other places in the Mediterranean, where the incompetence of the mainly Yank pilots had dropped them. So, the *History* fills in details of the accounts the survivors told us there, and they make an almost incredible story.

Some Horsas had to be flown from Cornwall to Morocco, a distance of some 1,400 miles non-stop across the Bay of Biscay, which was being patrolled by German aircraft. One crew had had to ditch on two occasions, first when the tow rope broke and secondly after an attack by a Condor aircraft. Another Horsa flew all the way with embedded in its wing a large and heavy piece of its undercarriage, which had bounced up from the runway on take-off.

For the build-up of glider strength in Africa, the American Waco (or Hadrian as we were supposed to call it) was shipped over in considerable quantities.[2] But the technicians were not shipped too, and our chaps had to set to and assemble the planes themselves, living the while in the crates in which the gliders had been received. One pilot who had the temerity to say that his self-assembled glider was not airworthy was threatened with RTU (Returned to Unit) and the officer test-flew it round the airstrip. Later, one glider lost its tail whilst flying over the Atlas Mountains. The two pilots and twelve passengers were of course all killed.

The *History* says that our party at Philippeville had 'been lost sight of for twelve days' and implies that this was why we missed the Sicily operation. I doubt this. It would not have been feasible for us to acclimatise ourselves to the Mediterranean high summer and to convert to Waco gliders in the time available.

Claude Smith does not record the night operation proposed for Rome which was all set up and then cancelled at forty-eight hours' notice – a pity, because it throws light on the state of the war at that time and would certainly have been a major event in the lives of those involved. He does tell of the voyage to Taranto on the *Princess Beatrix* and the Army's attempt to turn us into infantry in Italy, but unfortunately he does not give the who, how and why.

In May 1945 some of the Regiment did not come home. About thirty glider pilots were sent to India to raise a glider force there for use against the Japanese. Another group became the 'Independent Squadron', which stayed in the Med., having apparently a delightful time, living with the Yanks, ferrying gliders from place to place and eventually taking part in a relatively small operation in Southern France in August. Thereafter they went to Greece, not to fly but to form part of a peace-keeping force, an activity which cannot have been very pleasant.

The reason why I mention this unit (of whose existence I was only vaguely aware until I read the book) is that, had I reported sick at Putignano instead of soldiering on until I got on the troopship for home, I should in all probability have been posted to it on my recovery from jaundice. Thus, I would have missed – and honourably missed – the three North European operations and everything would have turned out very differently. I might well have ended up in India!

D-Day

The *History* states that 1,500 glider pilots were to be ready for the invasion of Europe. The Regiment was now a fully recognised part of the military machine.

For D-Day small sections of the Regiment were assigned to numerous tasks, some requiring only a handful of gliders, but each depending on the ability of the pilots to put down safely and in darkness on or near their objectives. From this distance in time the accounts of what these assignments were and how they were accomplished make extraordinary reading.

Security before D-Day being stringently applied, we had no knowledge and only a little inkling of what our comrades were being trained to do: all we knew about was what we were doing, and, as my account shows, we were not told until very late on what our task really was.

My unit in Operation Tonga, part of Operation Neptune, as the whole D-Day effort was called, required sixty-eight Horsas and four Hamilcars to land at LZ 'N' north of Ranville, Normandy, at 0300 hours on 6 June.[3] Claude Smith states that those that arrived were able to land along flare-paths. He also refers to some gliders 'unable to find room for themselves through those [anti-glider] poles'. Of course, this is absolute nonsense; our only landing aid was a single light indicating the turning point before our final run-in. From where we were it was impossible to see the poles, let alone find room among them.[4]

What I call the second lift was Operation Mallard, in which 248 gliders landed 3,200 troops plus guns and vehicles at 2100 hours on D-Day. This was the first time an armoured formation had been flown 200 miles directly into battle.

On D-Day thirty-four glider pilots were killed and many others injured, but the Regiment succeeded in 95 per cent of the many tasks it was given.

Observations on the Battle of Arnhem

A great deal has been written about Arnhem, one of the worst disasters to befall the British Army, held by some to be on a par with Gallipoli in the First World War, and doubtless there will be more in the years to come. As someone has pointed out, what was a defeat for us was a victory for the enemy, at a time when it was thought the war had practically been won. As this account is intended to be not only a personal memoir but also a minor footnote to history, I hope I may be excused if I add a few more general observations on the battle as I saw it.

One of the major controversies centres on the question of whether the airborne troops should have been put down at places 6 to 8 miles distant from their objective, the bridge. Had they been landed nearer they would undoubtedly have held the bridge longer, for more troops would have been available. In actual fact, the bridge was held for longer than had been planned; it was the failure of XXX Corps to capture Nijmegen Bridge and advance across it to relieve us that was the cause of the eventual disaster.

Could the 1st Airborne have held the whole town, also as originally planned, from a number of defensive positions around it? This would surely have depended on the extent and nature of the opposition. I have no recollection, as I have said, of being briefed on what reaction to the landings was to be expected, but Ryan says that officially 'troops of low category' (whatever that means) were all that were thought to be in the area.[5] It is difficult to think that anyone really believed this, and it is noticeable that *By Air to Battle*, the official account, says nothing about what is surely a vital point.

Arnhem was a major town and important communications centre. There was a large military airfield nearby, so well defended that it affected, if it did not dictate, the choice of LZs and DZs.[6] The Dutch were not quiescent under the occupation, far from it. For the purposes of suppression and protecting their own people, it was to be expected, regardless of the presence or absence of reliable intelligence information, that the Germans would have substantial forces there, quite apart from the possibilities of reinforcement from the Reich only a relatively few miles away.

Even if only 'low category troops' had been available, it seems to me, that a few low category troopers, with machine-guns well-sited in buildings and woods and under the sort of resolute command characteristic of the German Army, would have been enough to wreak havoc among even the best the airborne forces could put against them. The terrain of woodlands, gardens and streets of houses immensely favoured defence against attackers whose lines of advance had to be along roads and streets. Geoffrey Powell points out that his unit was more accustomed to exercising on the plains of India and of Wiltshire than to fighting among the buildings of a European town. We ourselves had had no training whatever in the techniques of street warfare.

Whether the presence of armour was anticipated or not is another part of the controversy. For many years a matter of surmise, the matter has conclusively been settled by Brian Urquhart (not to be confused with General Urquhart), who in his *A Life in Peace and War*, tells how aerial photography confirmed intelligence that two divisions of tanks were in the vicinity, and how this inconvenient information was deliberately suppressed, Urquhart himself being sent compulsorily on sick leave. His masters' minds were already made up and they did not want to be confused with the facts.[7]

A question that seems never to have been asked, then or since, is: what were we and the major portion of a large airborne force supposed to be doing in Oosterbeek when, not according to plan, we found ourselves there. Attacks were resisted where they were encountered and some minor, but costly, offensives were mounted, certainly, but having failed to get into the town, we were given no other role. It must have been obvious from the Monday night – it was pretty obvious to me – that the Germans' tactic was to stop any more of the invaders getting to where they could do most harm, i.e. into the town, and that they had in fact succeeded in this. Officially this was appreciated early on the Wednesday morning.[8]

Yet no other plan existed or was improvised to meet what must have been an obvious contingency. We could not get out to west, east or north, but the south, across the river, was, so far as I am aware, free from enemy. The wide river, it is true, presented a formidable obstacle, but it is a fact that a ferry was operating across it until that Wednesday morning. The failure to use the south side of the river as a landing area in the original operation, as an alternate route to the bridge, or even to assist the ground forces to link up with us, strikes me as incomprehensible.

Attempts were indeed made to get troops across the river eventually, but this was very late in the week and the movement was in the opposite direction, i.e. from south to north. Parties of Polish troops and from the Dorsets were indeed brought across in a futile attempt to reinforce us. But these expeditions dismally failed with great loss, because of the machine guns with which the enemy were now commanding the river.

I have since wondered if any assessment was made, in the light of this experience, of the appalling risk of ferrying some thousands of exhausted, disorganised and in some cases wounded men across the same stretch of water, where the transit of fresh organised troops had failed. Admittedly the rescue of some 2,000 men was no mean achievement, but to leave some uncounted hundreds to their own devices, all organisation and control abandoned, seems to me to be criminal. Yet no one was held responsible for these valuable lives, uselessly cast away.

The whole adds up to a bad plan inflexibly pursued. From first to last it smacks of casualness – casualness for which many men needlessly paid with their lives. Or, as Captain R.W. Thompson, a war correspondent, put it:

> The plain fact is that the 1st Airborne had been parachuted out upon a hopeless and impossible limb in accordance with a vain and irresponsibly optimistic plan, inadequately thought out.[9]

The palm for the most inane verdict on the battle must be awarded to General Montgomery, who declared that 'Market Garden was 90 per cent successful'.[10] This is tantamount to saying that a racehorse which leads the field and falls at the last fence is 90 per cent the winner. Arnhem was catastrophic both for the Airborne Division and for the unfortunate Dutch into whose area it was to descend. It had no redeeming features. It was an unforgivable disaster.

> The Arnhem tragedy had a deep and permanent effect on my attitude to life. Before it I had been trusting and relatively optimistic, with a self-confidence that was sometimes excessive. After it I doubted everything, tended to distrust my own as well as other people's judgement and became deeply sceptical about the behaviour of leaders. I never again could be quite convinced that great enterprises would go as planned or turn out well, or that wisdom and principle were a match for vanity and ambition.[11]

These are not my words: they were written by Brian Urquhart, the already-quoted intelligence officer whose efforts to warn his superiors of the impossible risk of the Arnhem operation were brushed aside. They are true for me too.

Evacuation from Arnhem

In his book *Bounce the Rhine!* Charles Whiting gives this extract from a report, source unidentified, of Canadian engineer Major Tucker:

> It was impossible to regulate the numbers of passengers carried by the boats at a time. Men panicked and stormed on to the boats, in some cases capsizing them. In many cases they had to be beaten off or threatened with shooting to avoid having the boats swamped. With the approach of dawn this condition became worse. They were so afraid that daylight would force us to cease our ferrying before they could be rescued.[12]

Whiting adds that men were drowned by the score.

But what, whilst this tragedy was going on, of the officers – those whose duty it traditionally was to look after the horses first, then the men and after that themselves? Of those who enjoyed an enhanced status and often luxurious living conditions so that they might the better carry out responsibilities not borne by the rank and file? The answer is, I do not know; I never saw any.

I was told later that they had grouped themselves at a little distance 'to give the men a chance', and I have a recollection of seeing such a group. If this is so, it was my misfortune to witness what sort of chance the men were given. To be fair, however, I should perhaps add that they were undoubtedly at the end, or beyond the end, of their tether too, and that the men would probably have shot anyone who tried to restore order amongst them at that time.

The conclusion of the matter is put by Chester Wilmot in his *The Struggle for Europe*:

> At daybreak on September 26th the evacuation had to stop, because German machine guns began sweeping the river. By then 2,163 men of the 1st Airborne Division and the Glider Pilot Regiment (together with 160 Poles and 75 Dorsets) had reached the safety of the south bank. Of the 10,000 who had landed north of the Neder Rijn only these few were rescued, and as near as can be told, 1,130 airborne troops remained in Arnhem for ever.[13]

Of what happened to the Glider Pilot Regiment another account states, '730 glider pilots, more than half those involved, were captured, killed or wounded at Arnhem'.[14]

General Urquhart's message

The text of General Urquhart's message to General Browning at I Airborne Corps HQ (prepared Sunday night, 24 September 1944):

> Urquhart to Browning. Must warn you unless physical contact is made with us early 25th Sept. consider it unlikely we can hold out long enough. All ranks now exhausted. Lack of rations, water, ammunition and weapons with high officer casualty rate. Even slight enemy offensive action may cause complete disintegration. If this happens all will be ordered to break towards the bridgehead, if anything, rather than surrender. Any movement at present in face of enemy impossible. Have attempted our best and will do so as long as possible.[15]

There seems to be an element of doubt as to whether the message was actually sent off. Ryan says it was encoded but gives no details of its transmission.[16] It appears in the message log of the 'Phantom Net' operator

('Phantom' was a small highly specialised force of observers reporting directly to the War Office in London). It is also referred to in General Montgomery's fulsome letter of congratulations to General Urquhart after the disaster.

Postscript to Arnhem

In 1997 I came across another book on the battle which gives it a different perspective. Written by a regular army officer, it shows, on the basis of German Army archives, how the battle looked and was conducted on their side.[17]

Although the reasons for the defeat given in most books are not without validity, the major factor was the incredibly swift and intelligent reaction to this wholly unexpected invasion on the part of the German commanders in the area, particularly Generals Student and Model (who had his HQ in Oosterbeek at that time).

Within hours they had organised every man (and some women) from all three services whom they could lay their hands on regardless of whether they were trained to fight or could even use weapons. These were directed to attack wherever they heard the sound of shooting, and speedily to form a barrier between the bulk of the airborne forces and the city. My comment about the use of low category troops is therefore not far from the mark.

Claude Smith refers to the sixteen (Golden says fifteen) airborne operations proposed and cancelled during the three months after D-Day. One of these seems to have had an influence on the one which was carried out shortly afterwards.

This was Comet, in which there would have been a major glider landing at Nijmegen, and 'coup-de-main' attacks on the other river crossings similar to those carried out in Normandy.[18] This having been planned and cancelled at short notice, the implication is that Market Garden was just an elaboration of it. If this is so, it may account for, but not excuse, the fact that Market Garden seemed just slung together.

Smith says that in anticipation of Comet, Albemarle/Horsa combinations were moved from Brize Norton to Manston, and that the cancellation took place no more than four hours before take-off time.

This does not fall in with my recollection, nor, I think, with the facts. No operation could have been cancelled within such a short time from take-off, without the pilots (tug and glider) having been briefed, the loads aboard and everything ready to go, and all of us knowing, and I have no recollection of any briefing or preparation. As my main account shows, we were down at Manston ten days before Market Garden, and it is the lackadaisical atmosphere down there that I particularly remember. I also think I was towed to Arnhem by Halifax. However, my memory may be faulty here.

Smith does not say much about the obvious defects of our part of Market Garden, although he was 'put in the bag' as a result of them. He does, however, confirm that it was indeed known that 'the enemy forces at Arnhem were formidable', and that the presence of the two refitting armoured divisions had been revealed, not only by air reconnaissance but via the top-secret Ultra signals intelligence, of which the achievements in this field were probably the single greatest contribution to victory. All this being definitely known, the sacrifice of a whole airborne division is all the more incomprehensible.[19]

Smith also says that of the 1,378 glider pilots who went in, 299 were killed and 469 wounded or made prisoner, a total of 768. Chatterton gives a different figure.[20]

Operation Varsity

Operation Varsity, the assault across the Rhine, was, according to the *History*, the largest single airborne lift ever made. It involved 40,000 para-troops and air-landing troops from both the British and the American armies. The entire force landed in the space of sixty-three minutes.[21] The Regiment provided the pilots to fly 440 gliders, and as my account shows, a large proportion, if not the larger proportion, was supplied by the RAF from flying-trained people who were at this stage in the war surplus to requirements.

Chatterton in his book seems to claim that the idea of using these pilots was entirely his own, and that he had had to persuade the Air Command to let him have them. In this he is totally contradicted by Claude Smith, who shows that, far from being reluctant, the RAF was desirous of taking over the whole responsibility for gliders and their crews.

It was as early as July 1944, i.e. just after the remarkable success of the airborne operations of D-Day, that the Air Ministry was pointing to the anomalous position where they had a large number of fully-trained pilots but were having to devote 1,500 of their personnel to train pilots from the Army.[22] The suggestion had been advanced that the Regiment should be disbanded in the interests of 'higher efficiency'! This proposition was only a continuation of the controversy attending the formation of the Regiment which I have mentioned earlier. Chatterton makes no mention that the matter had been long at issue: perhaps he had been kept in ignorance of it.

Operation Varsity was unusual in that it involved the large-scale use of airborne troops in a tactical role, i.e. the direct assault on enemy positions. Colonel Rock had envisaged two main tasks for gliders: coup-de-main attacks and reinforcement of ground already taken. Direct assault he described as 'charging the enemy in a fleet of RASC three-tonners'. The Regiment's activities and history would have been different had he lived. We among ourselves used to wonder why we were not used for trans-portation of people, petrol and other supplies to maintain the impetus of armoured spearheads. Claude Smith speculates on this too.[23]

The load I carried into Germany on this operation is correctly described as an RAF Forward Visual Control Post. There were two of them with the job of directing fighters on to enemy tanks and they accounted for sixteen kills in this battle.

RAF Glider Pilots

Although my account is in line with what we were led to believe, and follows what Chatterton wrote in his autobiography, the facts seem to be rather different.

According to Claude Smith's *History*, there had been, even in the early days, a body of opinion in the RAF that pilots should *ipso facto* be members of that force, which was devoting large resources, including whole air-fields, to their training and deployment. In the later stages of the war, it became illogical for the RAF to be giving flying training to Army people when they had a surplus of pilots-in-training of their own. Inter-service rivalry and empire building seems to have had a hand in it too.

It appears therefore that the conversion of potential aircrew to glider flying was not just Chattie's bright idea. Indeed, the reverse could have happened and we surviving GPR men might have ended up in the Royal Air Force.

A transfer in the opposite direction (so I read in the *Daily Telegraph* obituaries recently) did apparently take place when, also late in the war, some hundreds of the RAF Regiment (a force raised to defend airfields at home and abroad) were transferred to the Scots Guards. This was a tank regiment which saw much action in north-west Europe and sustained many casualties. I doubt the people involved were very happy about that.

In fairness I should add that the RAF intake got over their disquiet at having to associate with us after they had taken part in Operation Varsity. Some paid us the compliment of adopting the red beret, worn with RAF uniform, strictly contrary to regulations. But the RAF were always an undisciplined lot.

Last Words

There is nothing much to add to what I have written already. Those who stayed on in the Regiment were sent abroad to India and then to the unpleasant job of peace-keeping in Palestine, where they were treated as enemies by Jews and non-Jews alike. Some became air observation pilots or light liaison pilots, and some even took part in the Berlin airlift in 1949. Some served in Borneo, Malaya and Korea. I imagine these people had signed on as regulars.

The Regiment finally disbanded on 12 July 1957. Whilst I belong to the Regimental Association and both read and have contributed to *The Eagle*, its magazine, which provides fascinating information about what other people got up to, voluntarily or involuntarily, I do not attend reunions (I did go to one but did not in the least enjoy it) and could not bear to take part in remembrance services, which, involving berets, medals and banners, seem to be inseparable from them.

Nothing, it seems to me, can do justice to the tragedy, the excitement, the frustration, the loneliness, the rough good-fellowship and the desperation of what de Vigny aptly called '*Servitude et Grandeur Militaires*'.

Summer 1992

Notes

Introduction

1. The tow ropes on the Horsa were 3½ inches in diameter and about 100 yards long. They were attached to the nose on the Horsa Mk I, or the top of each wing via a Y-shaped yoke, on the Horsa Mk II. The earlier hemp tow ropes were liable to break and were later replaced with the more flexible nylon ropes, which contained a communications cable. According to Flight Lieutenant George Chesterton, who flew a Stirling over Normandy, Arnhem and on SOE missions, these communications cables 'seldom worked with any efficiency and instructions had to be bellowed for any chance of comprehension'. George Chesterton, *Also Flew* (Aspect Design, Malvern 2008), p. 78.
2. Unlike their US counterparts who were instructed to retire from the battle immediately.
3. All were manufactured in Britain except the Hadrian, which was built in the US and operated by the United States Army Air Force under the name of Waco CG-4A.
4. Due to the scarcity of original Horsa gliders, some museums have found they have to combine elements of these different marks to make one exhibit.
5. The Society's brief is to promote the memory and heritage of the Glider Pilot Regiment.
6. Articles included 'The Para who hitched a lift', *Portsmouth News*, 18 June 1997, and 'D-Day Memories from the Frontline', *The Guardian*, 5 June 2014.

Chapter 1: Beginnings – Joining the Royal Army Service Corps

1. RA comments: Nicknamed 'Alley Sloper's Cavalry', the Royal Army Service Corps had originally been called the Army Service Corps (ASC). It had derived its satirical nickname from one Alley Sloper, a character in a magazine popular early in the century.
2. Interestingly RA answers his CSM as 'Sir'. As a WO2, the CSM was usually addressed by subordinates as 'Sar'nt Major'.
3. Navy, Army, Air Force Institutes. This government-sponsored organisation ran non-profit-making canteens for the services. In the Second World War it was also responsible for ENSA, the entertainment organisation. In the main, it was staffed by members of the Royal Army Service Corps, supplemented by female civilian volunteers.

Chapter 2: Training – North of England

1. RA comments: In an obituary in the *Daily Telegraph*, 16 December 1993 (of Major Guy Knights MC), the Boyes rifle is described as 'one of the most ineffective weapons ever designed'.

2. RA comments: In this respect we got off lightly. Anthony Burgess (later well known as the author of *A Clockwork Orange*) was posted to an RAMC unit in the same 54th Division as ourselves. 'I tell you this is the end,' remarked his sergeant major. 'We were all pals when we formed in Luton in peacetime, and now they send us sods like you.'

3. RA comments: It must not be concluded that I engaged in these transient pleasures. I was too much afraid of getting VD (for which no effective medical cure existed at that time) or of being 'caught' and harried into marriage or maintenance on the grounds of alleged pregnancy.

Chapter 3: Training – South of England

1. RA uses a more modern term for conscription. The National Service (Armed Forces) Act 1939 imposed conscription on all males aged between 18 and 41 years old. The term 'national serviceman' was more commonly applied post-war to those males compelled to undertake, initially, eighteen months' military service from January 1949. The last national serviceman was discharged in 1963.

Chapter 6: The Hotspur Glider

1. The only operational role ever considered for the Hotspur was the carrying of equipment for the D-Day landings. The plan was never carried out.

2. The Westland Lysander was initially employed in the Second World War as a spotter and light bomber but suffered huge losses during the Battle of France in 1940. As RA comments, it later found fame when used by the Special Duties Squadron, delivering and recovering agents in occupied France, as well as rescuing shot-down airmen.

3. The Miles Magister had one advantage over the Tiger Moth – it had brakes.

Chapter 7: The Horsa Glider

1. Officially known as the 'cable angle indicator', this device was useful for night-flying or in fog, when the glider pilot could not see the tug aircraft in front. A dial with an illuminated vertical white line and a similar horizontal one was connected to the tow rope and set for optimum tug/glider elevation (slightly above or slightly below the tug). If the tow rope slackened, the glider pilot could correct his altitude so that the white lines married up again.

2. The Americans had some success in retrieving some of their gliders after operations both in Asia and Europe. If space and conditions allowed, a Dakota would trail a hook and 'snatch' a tow rope attached to the grounded glider. The towrope was looped and suspended off the ground by two poles.

Chapter 8: Overseas

1. Operation Ladbroke was a glider-borne assault on targets in the south-east of Sicily, part of the much larger Operation Husky which aimed to capture Sicily as a prelude to the invasion of Italy. British (1st Airborne) and US units took part in Ladbroke, but of the 136 Wacos and 8 Horsas committed to the night-time operation, some seventy gliders crashed into the sea, drowning over 250 men. Other gliders that did manage to surmount navigation errors or enemy flak landed miles from their targets. RA was indeed fortunate not to be included in this poorly planned disaster.

Chapter 9: D-Day, 6 June 1944

1. The brigade comprised Nos 3, 4 and 6 (Army) Commandos together with 45 (Royal Marine) Commando.
2. For a detailed narrative on this operation, see Kevin Shannon and Stephen Wright, *Operation Tonga: The Glider Assault, 6 June 1944* (Fonthill Media, London 2014).
3. Antony Beevor, *The Second World War* (Weidenfeld & Nicolson, London 2012), pp. 577–8.
4. Brigadier George Chatterton DSO, commander Glider Pilots.
5. Brigadier George Chatterton, *The Wings of Pegasus* (Macdonald, London, 1962), p. 112.
6. Along with the Wellington and Hampden bombers, the Whitley bomber was one of the three aircraft available to RAF Bomber Command at the outbreak of war, for tactical/medium bombing missions.
7. The Germans laid fields of larch poles, each approximately 10 inches in diameter and showing about 10 feet above the ground. They were often linked by wires or tripwires tied to grenades. While some gliders crashed into these obstacles and casualties resulted, most landing zones on D-Day were fortunately free of the 'asparagus fields'.
8. This bulldozer was most likely a US-manufactured Clarkair CA-1. It was compact and weighed only three tons, being designed as a glider-borne vehicle.
9. During the second day of the Allied invasion of Sicily, nervous US troops manning beachhead and offshore gun batteries at Gela fired on US transport planes carrying US paratroops. Large numbers of aircraft were shot down or severely damaged, resulting in hundreds of casualties.
10. RA met him again in 1997, see *Portsmouth News*, 18 June 1997.
11. Ministry of Information, *By Air to Battle: The Official Account of the British First and Sixth Airborne Divisions* (HMSO, London, 1945), p. 87. The bulldozer was to be employed in clearing the debris across the zone in preparation for subsequent landings.
12. RA comments: I have since learned from a postcard from the D-Day Museum at Southsea that 'he led the brigade across Pegasus Bridge and crossed Ranville Bridge playing Blue Bonnets over the Border'. As I was only a few hundred yards away from the canal bridge, my memory is probably correct.
13. This is a reference to Piper Bill Millin, Lord Lovat's piper. As elements of No. 1 Special Service Brigade crossed the two bridges, they lost several men to enemy snipers.
14. RA comments: His name was J.H. Nash and my memory was correct. In all, seven pilots from 'B' Squadron were killed. See *The Eagle*, April 1992, p. 98.
15. RA comments: The story of Johnny Thompson's head injury is confirmed by his first pilot, K.A. 'Taff' Evans, in a letter in *The Eagle* (August 1991, p. 7) commenting on an earlier one I had sent in.
16. At 2100 hours the HQ 6 Airlanding Brigade together with further infantry and recce units were delivered to landing zones 'N' and 'W'. This second lift involved 250 Horsas and Hamilcars.

17. Café Gondrée was owned by Georges and Thérèse Gondrée. Now run by their daughter Arlette, the café still operates besides Pegasus Bridge and has become a feature of recent D-Day commemorations.

Chapter 10: After D-Day

1. Golden, Lewis, *Echoes from Arnhem* (William Kimber, London, 1984), p. 96.
2. Chatterton, *Wings of Pegasus*, p. 131.
3. Golden, *Echoes from Arnhem*, p. 99.

Chapter 11: Arnhem

1. This 'Replacement Army' comprised drafts from depot staff, the police, and training schools and proved to be largely ineffective but the addition of 30,000 men from the Luftwaffe certainly bolstered the German defensive line.
2. Twenty-two of these gliders would become separated from their tugs, due to broken tow ropes, and would never make it beyond the English coast.
3. Nos 1 and 2 Wings the Glider Pilot Regiment were attached to the 1st Airborne Division. No. 1 Wing (HQ Harwell) commanded by Lieutenant Colonel I.A. Murray deployed three squadrons. Robert Ashby was in 'B' Squadron, normally based at Brize Norton but flew to Arnhem from Manston.
4. For a moving account of the desperate role of these Stirling squadrons at Arnhem, see Chesterton, *Also Flew*, pp. 100–9.
5. For a full Order of Battle and estimates of casualties, see Martin Middlebrook, *Arnhem 1944. The Airborne Battle* (Penguin Books, London 1994), pp. 439, 454–66.
6. Golden, *Echoes from Arnhem*, pp. 100, 105.
7. While Brussels was liberated on 3 September, it would take another nine days for the rest of Belgium to be cleared of German forces.
8. One weakness of the popular Smith & Wesson .38 revolver was the main spring, which, after constant use, often produced a weak hammer blow. This may have been the problem that Robert Ashby encountered.
9. Major Robert Cain, 2nd Battalion, South Staffordshire Regiment. After experiencing an abortive take-off from Manston when his Horsa glider's tow rope detached from the tug aircraft, Cain arrived near Arnhem on a later lift and was immediately involved in heavy fighting. Using PIATs, he repeatedly knocked out or disabled a number of enemy tanks and assault guns. For his valour he was awarded the Victoria Cross. His account of the fighting at Arnhem is held by the Airborne Assault Museum at the Imperial War Museum, Duxford.
10. Max Hastings, *Overlord* (Michael Joseph, London, 1984), pp. 223, 339.
11. The Glider Pilot Regiment remained under Army control, as distinct from the RAF.
12. The 75mm Pack Howitzer was a light (650kg), manoeuvrable piece designed for indirect fire, in contrast to the Quick-Firing 6-pounder and 17-pounder anti-tank guns. The howitzer and 6-pounder could be towed by a jeep and delivered by Horsa glider. The 17-pounder and its tow vehicle, the Morris Quad Field Artillery Tractor, required delivery via the more spacious Hamilcar glider. All were used at Arnhem by the 1st Airlanding Light Regiment, Royal Artillery.

13. Gliders were allocated a landing zone (LZ) while paratroopers endeavoured to land in a drop zone (DZ).
14. March is a market town in the Isle of Ely, Cambridgeshire.
15. Interestingly, Robert Ashby refers to his towing plane as a Halifax. Both 296 and 297 Squadrons, which did the bulk of the towing of the fifty-six Horsa gliders from Manston for the second lift, used the Armstrong Whitworth Albemarle transport aircraft.
16. Wolfheze is a village 10km north-west of Arnhem. The community had grown around a notable asylum, adjacent to the two landing zones. Unfortunately, the institution and neighbouring houses contained enemy units and were subjected to several bombing sorties by the USAAF, resulting in civilian casualties.
17. Golden, *Echoes from Arnhem*, p. 127. Golden was adjutant, 1st Airborne Division Signals.
18. This was one of the only two Hamilcars that overturned in the soft ground with the loss of their crews and two 17-pounder guns. A further Hamilcar crashed into the railway embankment. The pilots, who sat in tandem, were housed in a cockpit above the fuselage. If the glider pitched forwards on landing, the weight of the gun or tank inside would cause the craft to somersault, trapping both the pilots and the upturned crews.
19. Major Brian Urquhart (no relation to Major General 'Roy' Urquhart, commander 1st British Airborne Division), informed Lieutenant General 'Boy' Browning that intelligence had been received that the 9th and 10th SS Panzer Divisions were in the Arnhem area, and their presence would adversely affect the outcome of Operation Market Garden. Browning, Deputy Commander of First Allied Airborne Army, chose not to cancel or modify the operation and arranged for Urquhart to be sent home on medical grounds.
20. General Friedrich Kussin had been visiting one of his battalions based at Hotel Wolfheze. By chance, on his return journey into Arnhem, Kussin's driver came out of a road junction right into the forward body of men of the 3rd Parachute Battalion, who were advancing towards the Arnhem road bridge. Somewhat surprised by the staff car, they poured fire into it, unaware that they had claimed the town's commandant.
21. The plan envisaged the airborne forces being relieved by the arrival of XXX Corps within three days. As well as the Guards Armoured Division, the 43rd Wessex and 50th Northumbrian Divisions, the Corps could also call upon artillery and sappers to support the lightly armed airborne troops.
22. The Stirling was employed by the RAF as a heavy bomber between 1941 and 1943 when it was supplanted by the more versatile Lancaster and Halifax bombers. It was then adapted for use as a glider tug (Mk IV) to tow the Horsa and Hamilcar, as well as for the role of supply aircraft.
23. Revd Alastair Menzies, *Daily Telegraph*, 20 September 1994.
24. Urquhart, R.E., *Arnhem* (Cassel, London, 1958) pp. 123–4.
25. Golden, *Echoes from Arnhem*, p. 129.
26. Urquhart, *Arnhem*, pp. 121, 124.
27. Due to poor communications, General Urquhart went forward in a jeep to reconnoitre the progress of his men's advance but was cut off by the enemy. At his HQ,

command was devolved to his second in command for the three days of Urquhart's absence.

28. Powell, Geoffrey, *Men at Arnhem* (Leo Cooper, London, 1986), pp. 158–9.

29. British soldiers discovered a number of houses belonging to members of the Dutch National Socialist Party. The male collaborator invariably fled at the first sound of battle, often leaving a wife and children in the cellar.

30. The 'shot at dawn' penalty for military offences was removed by Act of Parliament in August 1930 for every crime except mutiny and treachery. Only four such executions were carried out in the whole of the Second World War. Sleeping on sentry duty had been a capital crime during the First World War.

31. Powell, *Men at Arnhem*, p. 219.

32. Kate ter Horst was an Arnhem resident, who tended over 200 wounded British troops at her house in Oosterbeek. They nicknamed her 'the Angel of Arnhem'.

33. The Independent Polish Parachute Brigade was formed in late 1941. Despite the original hopes of the Polish General Staff that the brigade would be used to capture provincial airfields in Poland, many Poles wanted the unit to be deployed to help the Warsaw Uprising in the late summer of 1944. Instead, the brigade was squandered at Arnhem.

34. The Bofors Gun was a widely used 40mm self-propelled anti-aircraft gun. Mounted on a commercial lorry chassis, it could be towed by carrier and was also light enough to be loaded into a glider.

35. *Daily Telegraph*, 2 September 1987. This term has now been renamed 'Post Traumatic Stress Disorder'.

Chapter 12: After Arnhem

1. Because the V2 was supersonic, it hit the ground and exploded faster than it took the sound waves of the rocket motor to reach a spectator.

Chapter 13: Operation Varsity

1. The First Canadian Army was Canadian-led but something of an international Army. It comprised, at various times, not only Canadian units but also British, US, Polish, Belgian Dutch and Czech brigades.

2. Although these two airborne divisions were part of the Second British Army, for the purposes of the Rhine crossing they came under the command of the US Army XVIII Airborne Corps.

3. The British part of the operation comprised 440 gliders, including 146 Horsa Mk I, 246 Horsa Mk II and 48 Hamilcar gliders. For full details of the air fleet, see 'Glider Pilot Regiment Operation Order', National Archives, Kew, London (hereafter TNA), WO 171/5128.

4. The combined Allied air armada comprised 1,696 aircraft bearing paratroops, 1,346 gliders carrying airlanding troops, vehicles and artillery, and 2,153 fighter escorts. See Devlin, Gerard, *Paratrooper! Saga of US Army and Marine and Glider Combat Troops during WWII* (St Martin's Press, New York, 1979), p. 616.

5. For a full report on enemy units, see Appendix F, Intelligence Summary No. 2, Headquarters the Glider Pilot Regiment, TNA, WO 171/5128. Most German divisions in the area were operating on less than a third of normal strength, while the 116 Panzer Division was estimated to possess only a dozen operating tanks. Nevertheless, German artillery, particularly the 88mm anti-aircraft guns, would inflict terrible casualties amongst the Allied airborne troops and their pilots.

6. The 6th Airlanding Brigade comprised the 12th Battalion The Devonshire Regiment, the 2nd Battalion Oxfordshire & Buckinghamshire Light Infantry, and the 1st Battalion Royal Ulster Rifles, together with airlanding light artillery and field ambulance units.

7. 'Statistics', The Glider Pilot Regiment, TNA, WO 171/5128.

8. Robert Ashby later recalled: In *The Eagle* magazine (vol. 8, No. 2, of December 1995) there is a photograph of one of the oaks on the Marks Hall Estate. It is 700 years old. My thoughts about the scenes my tree had witnessed were probably not far out. Long after the war, I found that I was not nearly the only one to have acted thus: 'The nearness of victory gave danger a special edge. The more experienced the pilots ... the more tense they were. Captain Rex Norton had sat up writing letters until late at night ... For some there was a strong need to be alone ... Others walked in the gloom that morning around and around the inside perimeter of the airfield until it began to get light.' Alan Lloyd, *The Gliders* (Secker & Warburg, London, 1982), p. 182.

9. Because of the ground smoke, all seventy-two of the C-46 aircraft dropped the entire US 513th Parachute Infantry into the British glider zone. See Devlin, *Paratrooper!*, p. 620.

10. Ministry of Information, *By Air to Battle*, p. 143.

11. A similar fate befell Lieutenant Colonel 'Jeff' Nicklin, commander of the 1st Canadian Parachute Battalion, part of the 3rd Parachute Brigade. Having survived a similar 'snag' on D-Day, during Operation Varsity his parachute caught on a tall tree and as he tried to cut himself free, he was shot dead. *Toronto Daily Star*, 31 March 1945.

12. The glider floor and undercarriage would sometimes disintegrate during a rough landing. Consequently, the airborne forces were trained to brace for impact by belting up, lifting their legs and linking arms. In the event of sudden combustion, the men would perish in a compacted mass.

13. Ministry of Information, *By Air to Battle*, p. 143.

14. Lloyd, *The Gliders* , p. 209.

15. Captain (Harold) Rex Norton, killed in action 24 March 1945, aged 23 years old. Buried Reichswald Forest War Cemetery, Germany.

Chapter 15: Epilogue and Reflections

1. Claude Smith, *The History of the Glider Pilot Regiment* (Leo Cooper, London, 1992).

2. The CG-4A Waco was the most widely used glider during the Second World War. At 20ft shorter than the Horsa, its capacity was considerably less, carrying up to fifteen troops compared to the Horsa's twenty-eight. But the Waco was more robust and could be landed in a smaller zone.

3. Smith, *History of the Glider Pilot Regiment*, p. 92.

4. Ibid, p. 98.
5. Ryan, Cornelius, *A Bridge Too Far* (Hamish Hamilton, London, 1974), pp. 68, 95.
6. Ministry of Information, *By Air to Battle*, p. 97.
7. Brian Urquhart, *A Life in Peace and War* (Harper Collins, London 1987), p. 27.
8. Urquhart, *Arnhem*, p. 103.
9. Whiting, *Bounce the Rhine!*, p. 14.
10. Powell, *Men at Arnhem*, p. 32.
11. Urquhart, *A Life in Peace and War*, p. 76.
12. Whiting, *Bounce the Rhine!*, p. 8.
13. Chester Wilmot, *The Struggle for Europe* (William Collins, London 1952), pp. 582–3.
14. Lloyd, *The Gliders*, p. 163.
15. Philip Warner, *Phantom* (Kimber, London, 1982), Appendix 2.
16. Ryan, *A Bridge Too Far*, p. 428.
17. Kershaw, Robert J., *It Never Snows in September* (Crowood Press, Ramsbury, 1990).
18. Smith, *History of the Glider Pilot Regiment*, p. 102.
19. Ibid,, p. 106.
20. Chatterton, *Wings of Pegasus*, pp. 107, 122.
21. Smith, *History of the Glider Pilot Regiment*, p. 131.
22. Ibid,, p. 103.
23. Ibid,, p. 123.

Bibliography

Allen, Peter, *One More River. The Rhine Crossing of 1945* (Charles Scribner & Sons, New York, 1980).

Anonymous (Louis Hagen), *Arnhem Lift. Diary of a Glider Pilot* (Pilot Press, London, 1945).

Beevor, Anthony, *Arnhem. The Battle for the Bridges* (Viking, London, 2018).

Chatterton, Brigadier George, *The Wings of Pegasus* (Macdonald, London, 1962).

Chesterton, George, *Also Flew* (Aspect Design, Malvern, 2008).

Cole, Lieutenant Colonel Howard, *On Wings of Healing. The Story of the Airborne Medical Services* (William Blackwood, Edinburgh, 1963).

Devlin, Gerard, *Paratrooper! Saga of US Army and Marine and Glider Combat Troops during WWII* (St Martin's Press, New York, 1979).

Golden, Lewis, *Echoes from Arnhem* (William Kimber, London, 1984).

Hibbert, Christopher, *The Battle of Arnhem* (Batsford, London, 1962).

Kershaw, Robert, *It Never Snows in September* (Crowood Press, Ramsbury, 1990).

Lloyd, Alan, *The Gliders* (Secker & Warburg, London, 1982).

Mead, Richard, *General 'Boy'. The Life of Lieutenant General Sir Frederick Browning* (Pen & Sword, Barnsley, 2010).

Middlebrook, Martin, *Arnhem 1944. The Airborne Battle* (Viking, London, 1994).

Ministry of Information, *By Air to Battle: The Official Account of the British First and Sixth Airborne Divisions* (HMSO, London, 1945).

Morrison, Will, *Horsa Squadron* (William Kimber, London, 1988).

Powell, Geoffrey, *Men at Arnhem* (Leo Cooper, London, 1986).

Rottman, Gordon, *World War II Glider Assault Tactics* (Osprey, Oxford, 2014).

Ryan, Cornelius, *A Bridge Too Far* (Hamish Hamilton, London, 1974).

Seton, Albert, *The Fall of Fortress Europe 1943–45* (Batsford, London, 1981).

Urquhart, Brian, *A Life in Peace and War* (Weidenfeld & Nicolson, 1987).

Urquhart, R.E., *Arnhem* (Cassell, London, 1958).

Warner, Philip, *Phantom* (Kimber, London, 1982).

Whiting, Charles, *Bounce the Rhine!* (Leo Cooper, London, 1952).

Wilmot, Chester, *The Struggle for Europe* (Wm Collins, London, 1952).

Index